# NOAH WEBSTER

# NOAH WEBSTER

## Man of Many Words

CATHERINE REEF

**CLARION BOOKS**
HOUGHTON MIFFLIN HARCOURT
BOSTON   NEW YORK

Clarion Books
215 Park Avenue South
New York, New York 10003

Clarion Books is an imprint of Houghton Mifflin Harcourt Publishing Company.

www.hmhco.com

The text was set in 12-point Minister.
Map illustrations by Kristine A. Lombardi

Library of Congress Cataloging-in-Publication Data
Reef, Catherine.
Noah Webster : man of many words / Catherine Reef.
pages cm
Summary: A biography on Noah Webster, a controversial political activist, the primary shaper of the American
language, and author of the Blue-Backed Spellers and the famous dictionary that bears his name. Illustrated
with black-and-white archival images.—Provided by publisher.
ISBN 978-0-544-12983-2 (hardback)
1. Webster, Noah, 1758–1843—Juvenile literature. 2. Lexicographers—United States—Biography—Juvenile
literature. 3. Educators—United States—Biography—Juvenile literature. I. Title.
PE64.W5R44 2015
423.092—dc23
[B]
2014027803

Manufactured in China
SCP 10 9 8 7 6 5 4 3 2 1
4500530697

*For John S. Reef, an astute observer of language*

*Life is short, and every hour should be employed to good purposes.*

— Noah Webster

# Contents

# BEGIN'NING

noun. that which is first.

NOAH WEBSTER dressed by starlight. Black trousers, black stockings, black coat—he wore the stern clothes of a proper New Englander. He was six feet tall, a sturdy oak of a man. Yet he walked gently through the sleeping house. He entered his second-floor study and closed the door just as the first, weak rays of sunlight filtered through the window. The comet that was visible in the night sky, the great comet of 1807, was fading with the dawn.

Webster picked up his spectacles from the circular table that served as his desk and put them on his face. He rubbed his strong hands together, burnishing them against November's chill. He had spent many hours in this room, sealed off from the happy sounds of family life. "I am not formed for society," he once wrote. "The reflections of my own mind"

Noah Webster sits at a table, surrounded by his beloved books,
in this illustration from an 1879 edition of his dictionary.

were better companions, he said. He irritated others, and he knew it. Even men who had never met Webster called him an "incurable lunatic" and a "spiteful viper."

What had he done to make these people so upset? He had written.

Noah Webster had stirred up controversy by writing books and articles about politics and language.

He had called for a strong federal government when the United States was a brand-new nation unsure of its future. People were deeply divided on the issue, with many insisting that power belonged not to a central government, but to each of the thirteen states. "America is an independent empire, and ought to assume a national character," Webster wrote. "So long as any individual state has power to defeat the measures of the other twelve, our pretended union is but a name, and our confederation, a cobweb." He urged his fellow citizens to think of themselves as Americans rather than as Virginians, New Yorkers, Pennsylvanians, or residents of his own state, Connecticut.

Webster claimed that English, as spoken and written in the United States, could be a force that brought people together. "It is the business of *Americans*," he stated, "to diffuse an uniformity and purity of *language,* —to add superiour dignity to this infant Empire and to human nature." He wanted the language to embrace purely American words, such as *skunk* and *moccasin*. He hoped, too, to streamline spelling, to have Americans write *wagon* and not *waggon,* and *theater* rather than *theatre.* American English was different from British English, Webster insisted, and it ought to be a source of national pride. These notions hardly seem strange today, but when he published his ideas in the 1780s, Webster exposed himself to ridicule. His critics asked one another, *What will "this oddity of literature" think of next?*

People laughed, but Webster never doubted himself. On this morning, at age forty-nine, he was beginning the greatest project of his life, one his critics called folly. He planned to write a dictionary, the largest and most comprehensive dictionary of the English language ever compiled. It would be an American dictionary, based on his strong opinions, which were the product of many years of thought. He opened a clean notebook, lifted his quill pen, and wrote: "*A* is the first letter of the Alphabet in most of the known languages of the earth. . . ."

# CHAPTER 1

# A BOY WHO DREAMED OF BOOKS AND WORDS

THE LETTER *A* is one kind of beginning; birth is another. Noah Webster, Jr., was born in the West Division of Hartford, Connecticut, in his family's farmhouse, on October 16, 1758. Like his brothers and sisters, Noah was born in the best room, the one that served as a parlor during the day and his parents' bedchamber at night. This room was furnished simply, with straight-backed chairs and a four-poster bed. A massive stone fireplace offered heat, and a black Bible sat on the writing desk, ready to be consulted. The Websters sought its guidance for even the simplest duties of daily life.

Noah's mother, Mercy Steele Webster, had a great-great-grandfather who sailed to Plymouth Colony on the *Mayflower* in search of religious freedom. Like all farm women, Mercy Webster worked hard, making cloth, sewing and mending clothes, cooking and preserving food, gardening, and sweeping out the house. Somehow she had time to school the children in spelling and arithmetic. She read to them and taught them to play the flute. Beauty touched her soul, and she cried easily if she happened on a heartfelt phrase in a book or heard a well-loved melody. She passed along her loves to Noah. As a young man, he would turn to his books and flute whenever he felt low. In his diary he marveled that "the sound of a little hollow tube of wood should dispel in a few moments, or at least alleviate, the heaviest cares of life!"

Mercy Webster led the family in singing psalms every night. As good colonial parents, the Websters made their home a godly setting, to start

Noah Webster's childhood home, shown here in a picture from 1912, was restored in the 1960s and opened as a museum.

the children on the path to salvation. Mercy's husband, Noah Webster, Sr., had little formal schooling, but he was a bright man whose mind was open to new ideas. He was a founder of the local First Book Society, an early version of a public library. He served as a church deacon and justice of the peace.

Hartford in the 1750s was one of Connecticut's two capitals; New Haven was the other. Hartford was a growing town, where twenty or more shops lined the main street, selling everything from sugar, tea, and flour to gunpowder, nails, and axes. Some merchants were so eager for profits that they built shops on top of Hartford's old burial ground, which had been set aside as a graveyard in 1640. Others moved their businesses closer and closer to the road. In 1758, the year Noah was born, Hartford's leaders halted this inching forward by ordering property owners in the center of town to put in brick sidewalks.

Nearly all of the town's thirty-nine hundred people had English roots. About a hundred were African Americans, most of them enslaved. Slavery was legal throughout the colonies, although large-scale slaveholding never took hold in New England as it did in the South. A prosperous Connecticut family might own a slave or two, or possibly three.

In 1636, English settlers purchased the land that became the West Division from the Saukiog Indians. Generations of Saukiog had lived beside the Connecticut River, which teemed with fish. They hunted game and gathered nuts and berries in nearby forests and meadows. The Saukiog continued to live close to the West Division after the English

The Puritan leader Thomas Hooker, remembered as the "father of Connecticut," founded Hartford in 1636 with about a hundred followers, including at least one of Noah Webster's ancestors.

came, because having armed settlers nearby offered protection from their enemies, the Pequot and Mohegan tribes.

In this setting, young Noah grew into a lanky boy. His gray eyes were flecked with brown, and his red hair never would behave. As soon as he was big enough, he joined his father and older brother, Abraham, in the fields. The boys pushed a plow and sowed seeds in spring, pulled weeds throughout the summer, and gathered the ready crops come fall. All children worked hard on a colonial farm, boys and girls alike. Noah's sisters, Mercy and Jerusha, churned butter, gathered eggs, and spun linen and wool. They also looked after the youngest child, Charles, who was born in 1762. At night the children slept on straw mattresses, the boys in one of two upstairs rooms and the girls in the other.

Between the fall harvest and spring planting, the children attended the South Middle School. In colonial Connecticut, towns of seventy or more households were required to provide a school for half the year. Most of these "common schools" were small buildings where children of all ages sat together on backless benches. Pupils had few supplies or textbooks. Some families owned *The New-England Primer,* which was first published around 1690. This reader offered simple verses on religious themes for children to read and learn by heart.

*The New-England Primer,* published in Boston in the late 1600s, was the first beginning reader intended for American children.

Another book, *A New Guide to the English Tongue,* by the British author Thomas Dilworth, came into use in the 1740s. Dilworth's book began with the alphabet and moved on to tables of two-letter syllables for pupils to memorize: "ba be bi bo bu." Next came words of two and three letters, followed by simple religious readings:

*No Man may put off the Law of God.*
*The Way of God is no ill Way . . .*

Teaching religion in school was just as important as teaching reading, colonial leaders believed. Children needed faith to protect them from "that ould deluder, Satan."

Women taught in some small-town schools, but most colonial teachers were men. Schoolmasters needed no training, so just about any man could keep school. Some schoolmasters had college degrees, but many were drifters, drunkards, or indentured servants who had agreed to teach for a period of years if the community paid their passage from England. Towns wanting to get the most for their money often expected the teacher to serve in other ways, perhaps by leading the choir, cleaning the church, or digging graves. Keeping school was a tedious, low-paying job, so teachers tended to drift away as easily as they came. Indentured schoolmasters were known to run off to avoid serving their full term of service. In 1777, one Connecticut town offered a reward for the return of its schoolmaster, a man "of a pale complexion, with short hair" who had "the itch very bad, and sore legs."

For Noah Webster, school meant boredom. During the months when school was in session, he spent five or six hours each day "in idleness, in cutting tables and benches in pieces," he said, "or perhaps in some roguish tricks."

Noah learned no history in school, although he was growing up in a momentous time. In 1754, four years before he was born, Great Britain and France went to war in North America to decide which nation would control the continent and its profitable fur trade. At the time the war broke out, nearly all land east of the Mississippi River had been

This early American cartoon pokes fun at the ignorance of the typical schoolmaster.

claimed by Britain or France. The French had settled along the St. Law-rence and Mississippi Rivers and in some of the northern territory that would become Canada. They were greatly outnumbered by the English, whose colonies ran along the East Coast, between the Atlantic Ocean and the Appalachian Mountains. As English settlers began to push west, the French built forts, hoping to stop them. Borders were vague, though, and each of the two powers claimed the Ohio River valley as its own.

Native people battled on both sides of this conflict, which is known as the French and Indian War. Colonial militiamen fought for the British, and among them was Noah's father. Leaving his wife to run the farm, he helped defend Fort William Henry, a British outpost on Lake George, in New York. In August 1757, the fort came under such heavy bom-bardment that the British and Americans had to give it up. The French promised no harm to the defeated force, but many looked the other way while their Indian allies brutally attacked the British and colonists. No one was safe, not the sick and wounded, not the women and children who had been sheltered in the fort, not the Indians and free blacks who had fought on the British side. Hundreds were hacked to death, scalped alive, or taken prisoner. "This horrid scene of blood and slaughter obliged our officers to apply to the French Guard for protection, which they refus'd," wrote a Massachusetts colonel who lived to tell the tale. Noah Webster, Sr., felt grateful to make it home alive.

A series of British victories in 1758 and 1759 led to the surrender of Quebec, the French capital in North America. The treaty ending the war, signed in Paris in 1763, gave all French land east of the Mississippi to

In this nineteenth-century wood engraving, the French general Louis-Joseph de Montcalm tries to stop his Native American allies from attacking British and American soldiers and civilians leaving Fort William Henry.

Great Britain. When news of the treaty reached Hartford, the town erupted in celebration. People lit bonfires, set off fireworks, and rang church bells for an hour.

Trouble was just beginning for the colonists, though. Maintaining a fighting force so far from home had cost Great Britain a huge amount of money. Even with the war won, Britain planned to station ten thousand soldiers on the western frontier, near the Appalachian Mountains, to protect settlers there. The British government, under King George III, hoped to replenish its treasury by taxing the colonists. In 1765, Britain's Parliament passed the Stamp Act, a law that placed a tax on every piece of printed paper used in the colonies, from deeds and mortgages to newspapers, pamphlets, and playing cards. The fee was small, but colonists objected to it on principle. Taxes like this one amounted to British treachery. How dare the mother country tax them without their approval? Since the time the colonies were founded, their legislatures — not Parliament — had raised the taxes that colonists paid. If the Stamp Act was allowed to stand, what would Parliament tax next?

In Boston, a citizens' alliance known as the Sons of Liberty ransacked the homes of British appointees and hung the tax master in effigy. In October 1765, a group calling itself the Stamp Act Congress petitioned Parliament and the king to repeal the hated tax. American merchants began boycotting British goods, and trade between Britain and America came to a halt. Soon, British exporters were losing so much business that they too demanded an end to the tax. Faced with angry protests on both sides of the Atlantic, Parliament repealed the Stamp Act in March 1766.

Yet there were more taxes and outrages to come. Beginning in 1767, Britain put in place the Townshend Acts, which imposed duties on imported glass, lead, paper, and tea. They allowed British authorities to search colonial homes and businesses for smuggled goods, and they denied a trial by jury to anyone violating these acts. Boston retaliated by refusing to import any British goods on which duties had been placed.

Britain stationed infantrymen in Boston, which only caused tension to mount. On March 5, 1770, red-coated British soldiers fired into a jeering crowd, killing five Americans and wounding six others. The incident is remembered as the Boston Massacre.

In time Noah Webster, Jr., would have a great deal to say about the events of his day, but as a boy he liked to steal away from his father's fields and spend hours in the shade of an apple tree, reading books and thinking about the words in them. What did they mean, exactly? How did they fit together to form sentences and express ideas? If his father tracked him down, Noah received a scolding and a swift order: Back to work!

Noah loved music almost as much as he loved books. When he was twelve he formed a singing group with his friends from neighboring farms. On Sundays the boys sat together in church and practiced their harmonies while singing hymns. Noah was shocked when churchgoers sitting near them complained about the noise. Convinced that the criticism was unfair, he defended himself and his friends in Hartford's newspaper, the *Connecticut Courant.* Claiming to have a "considerable degree of knowledge in the art of Music," he explained that the boys meant no harm; they hoped singing would teach them obedience and good manners. But did they receive support from their fellow churchgoers? They did not, he wrote. Instead, they met with opposition "from the envious and ilnatur'd." This unsigned letter from August 1771 was Noah Webster's first published writing.

Noah's family worshiped at the Fourth Church of Christ, a large, plain meetinghouse. In October 1772, the church welcomed a new minister. Nathan Perkins was young, just twenty-four, but he was learned. He had graduated with distinction from the College of New Jersey (now Princeton University). A small, stocky man with a big voice, Perkins was

British soldiers fire on Bostonians on March 5, 1770. The five colonists killed that day are considered the first Americans to die in the struggle for independence from British rule.

"an intelligent and agreeable companion," said one of his lifelong friends, a minister named Daniel Waldo. "He was always ready to converse on any subject, and was particularly at home on subjects connected with Theology." Waldo added, though, that Perkins "rarely indulged in sallies of wit." Serious Mr. Perkins "was eminently devoted to the interests of his flock. He visited them frequently and familiarly, and was regarded by them all as their common friend."

Perkins gave sermons on "sinless perfection," which he said was impossible to achieve. He lectured on "the right way to understand the inspired writings." As Noah listened to Perkins speak, he saw a future for himself that had nothing to do with tilling the soil. He wanted to be an educated man—to go to Yale College, in New Haven.

When Noah told his father about his dream, the older man hesitated. He knew that Noah loved to learn, and how proud he would have been to have a son graduate from Yale! But how could he afford to send young Noah to college? The tuition, room, and board would cost about twenty-five pounds a year. This was a huge sum to a farmer who could not spend ten pounds for a second horse. Noah Webster, Sr., thought the matter over, weighing the pros and cons. If Noah went to Yale, the family would struggle financially. Land had value, though, and if strapped for cash, Noah Senior could mortgage his farm. Besides, it would be impossible for all three of his sons to take over the farm one day; it was simply too small. It made sense for Noah to do something else with his life. When Noah Senior gave his son an answer, it was yes.

This was happy news for young Noah, but it meant that hard work lay ahead. To be admitted to Yale, he had to pass an examination in Latin, classical Greek, mathematics, and the rules of poetry. He would never learn all he needed to know at the South Middle School; but luckily for Noah, Nathan Perkins agreed to be his tutor. Youths planning to go to college often studied under a minister's guidance. There was no set amount of time for preparation, just as there was no usual age for entering college. A young man went when he was ready.

No women went to college in the eighteenth century. Most people believed that women should learn to read the Bible but that too much study drew their attention away from home and family. People also thought that studying might harm women's brains.

Over the next two years, Noah met often with Perkins and spent every spare minute learning on his own. At last, when he was nearly sixteen, Perkins handed him a certificate stating that his scholarly achievements and high moral character made him fit to enter Yale. Perkins would spend sixty-six years as a pastor in the West Division of Hartford. He would help more than a hundred young men prepare for college, but Noah Webster was the first. Like all the best teachers, he taught his students the joy of learning. Decades later, when Webster read of Perkins's death, he noted, "To his instruction and example I am somewhat indebted for my taste for the study of languages."

In September 1774, Noah said goodbye to his friends and loved ones, and embarked with his father on the forty-mile journey south to New Haven, on the Connecticut coast. Because the Websters had only one horse, father and son took turns riding and walking. After Noah Junior proved to the Yale faculty that he was worthy of admission, Noah Senior traveled home alone.

# CHAPTER 2

# COLLEGE IN WARTIME

THE STREETS of New Haven formed nine neat squares that pleased Noah Webster's sense of order. There was a public green at the center, one of the largest in New England. Gulls cried in the clean, brisk sky over New Haven's harbor as winds filled the sails of ships bound for Boston, New York City, and the far-off West Indies.

Amid such lovely tidiness, Yale College was an eyesore. No trees grew on the campus. Anyone could see that the earliest of Yale's buildings, Old College, was falling apart. Back in 1750, twenty-four years before Noah Webster arrived on the scene, a British traveler noted that Old College was "very much decayed." Since then, Yale's trustees had never found the money to fix it.

The forty freshmen slept two to a tiny room in Connecticut Hall, a building that was freezing in winter and hot as a baker's oven in summer. It was no wonder the students called Connecticut Hall the "Brick

Students and faculty stroll outside the buildings of Yale College in this print from 1786.

Prison." Ranging in age from twelve to twenty, the freshmen were the lowliest students at Yale. They wore plain street clothes while the upperclassmen walked about in black gowns. They chopped firewood and ran errands for the sophomores, juniors, and seniors, and always addressed them as "sir." If an upperclassman wanted to pass through a doorway, a freshman had to step aside and let him go first.

Yale was founded in 1701 to train clergymen for colonial churches, but by 1774 most of the students wanted to be lawyers or physicians. The freshmen and sophomores worked hard to master Latin, Greek, mathematics, and religion. Natural philosophy—the science of nature and the universe—awaited them in their junior year. The curriculum was meant to discipline the mind, but by the 1770s it was coming under fire. Latin and Greek were "of no advantage to the common purposes of life," objected the Connecticut poet John Trumbull, who was a tutor at Yale. America was young and unfinished and needed everyone to pitch in. The colonists wanted their colleges to impart knowledge that graduates could use every day in their work and community. The teaching of English grammar, a new subject at Yale, was a first step in this direction.

Once or twice a week the students heard lectures by professors in black robes and wigs, but most of their instruction came from tutors. Yale assigned one tutor to each freshman class, to guide the young men through all four years of college. Noah Webster's class tutor, the Reverend Joseph Buckminster, was a kindhearted, scholarly man. "His mind was rapid in its operations, and impatient of delay. His imagination was excursive, and ever on the wing," said a fellow minister who knew him well. "Frankness and honesty were traits in his character, which all, who knew him, must have observed and admired." If a young man had something on his mind, Buckminster was willing to listen. He rejoiced with the students when they did well, but when he was alone he gave in to depression, to "deep gloom of mind."

Three times a day, Buckminster listened to Noah and his classmates recite their lessons. The students also took part in disputations, which were debates on religion or science. And they gave declamations, or speeches, in English or in one of the ancient languages. Their teachers thought that debating and declaiming made the young men better thinkers.

The students ate together and complained constantly about the food. "Injun" pudding, a concoction made from cornmeal and molasses, was the usual fare at dinner, the midday meal. There might also be potatoes, cabbage, broth, a small serving of meat, and metal tankards of cider to wash it all down. Noah much preferred the brown bread and milk served in the evening at supper.

Yale's students were an unruly bunch known to toss beef bones at their professors during dinner. To keep them in line, the faculty insisted they buy a copy of *The Laws of Yale-College* and have it with them at all times. "All the Scholars are required to live a religious and blameless Life according to the Rules of God's Word," this book declared. Any student who missed daily prayers had to pay a penny. A student could also be fined for breaking any number of college laws, some of which seem funny or strange today. He was not to leave his room without permission. Neither was he allowed to fight, be drunk or idle, sing during study time, or wear women's clothing. For offenses such as cursing, robbery, and getting married, a student would be expelled.

Noah made lasting friendships at Yale. His best friend, Joel Barlow, had grown up on a farm in the town of Redding, in southeastern Connecticut. Joel was outgoing and loved to laugh. At twenty, he was four years older than Noah, but he was a freshman too. He had friends in New Haven and made sure Noah was invited to their dances, knowing how Noah loved to dance. Joel sometimes took Noah out drinking, and he taught his younger friend to swear. Other freshmen envied Noah's daring.

Together Noah and Joel joined the Brothers in Unity, a student club that held debates and put on plays. In Noah's junior year the Brothers in Unity presented *The West Indian,* a popular comedy about a plantation owner from a Caribbean island who travels to England. (The British were quick to laugh at a West Indian, an Irishman, or any other foreigner.)

Webster's friendship with his Yale classmate Joel Barlow, pictured here, was to endure for decades.

What part Noah Webster played in the production is unknown.

According to *The Laws of Yale-College,* "If any Scholar shall any where act a Comedy or Tragedy, he shall be fined three Shillings, one Shilling if he shall be present at the acting of one." But Yale's president, Nephtali Daggett (a man the students called "Old Tunker"), allowed the Brothers in Unity to stage their plays.

A noble feeling—the yearning for liberty—drew Webster and Barlow into a student militia group that formed in February 1775. As the hundred or so new militiamen practiced marching and handling firearms, shouts of "Poise your firelock, cock your firelock!" were commonly heard at Yale. Relations between Great Britain and the North American colonies were growing more hostile by the day, so like many colonists, the young men at Yale were readying for war.

Parliament had repealed most provisions of the Townshend Acts in

April 1770, but Britain still taxed tea in the colonies, and this angered many people. In December 1773, three British ships laden with tea sat in Boston Harbor because the citizenry refused to let the cargo be unloaded. On the calm, quiet night of December 16, fifty or more colonists boarded the vessels. Many had disguised themselves as Mohawk Indians to keep their identities secret. Over the next three hours, they made "a little salt-water tea," throwing the entire cargo—all three hundred forty-two chests—into the harbor.

The Boston Tea Party so infuriated the British that punishing Boston was not enough. The entire colony of Massachusetts was made to pay for this rash exploit. Britain closed the busy port of Boston to oceangoing vessels. It forbade the people of Massachusetts to hold town meetings and required them to quarter British soldiers in their homes. These laws were outrageous; in fact, they were intolerable. So that is what the colonists called them: the Intolerable Acts.

The thirteen colonies responded as one. In September 1774, as Noah Webster was learning his way around Yale, fifty-six colonial delegates convened in Philadelphia. Silas Deane, a Connecticut delegate, informed his wife that he reached Philadelphia "in high spirits, if it is possible to be really so when the eyes of millions are upon us." He and the others drafted a document, the Declaration of Rights and Grievances. Addressed to the king, it outlined the "impolitic, unjust, and cruel" treatment they had endured. The delegates also called for a boycott of British goods until the Intolerable Acts were repealed. This gathering in Philadelphia is known as the First Continental Congress. Satisfied that they had done everything they could to end the conflict peacefully, the delegates agreed to meet again in the spring.

But peace was not to be enjoyed. Instead, Great Britain stationed some thirty-five hundred soldiers in Massachusetts. Companies of colonial farmers and tradesmen known as minutemen remained alert and ready to pick up guns and fight against the British with a minute's notice. When the British general Thomas Gage learned that the Americans were gathering arms and ammunition in Concord, Massachusetts, he ordered eight hundred of his soldiers to seize the store of weapons. On the morning of April 19, 1775, the advance guard of this fighting force exchanged gunfire with minutemen in the town of Lexington, leaving eight Americans dead. The British marched on to Concord, but the colonists

British soldiers and American militiamen exchanged their first gunfire in Lexington, Massachusetts, on April 19, 1775.

were waiting for them there. Both sides lost men in battle that day, but British losses were greater.

News of the battles at Lexington and Concord took two days to reach Yale. The stunning reports "filled the country with alarm, and rendered it impossible for us to pursue our studies to any profit," noted a sophomore named Ebenezer Fitch. Who could focus on Latin, knowing that militiamen had chased the British back to Boston and were keeping up their siege? Led by a local druggist named Benedict Arnold—this was the same Benedict Arnold who later betrayed his country—some of the older students raided a British ammunition storehouse. The students then took off for Boston to fight beside their countrymen. Yale's campus was in such disorder that President Daggett sent everyone home until the end of May.

By the time classes resumed, the Second Continental Congress was meeting in Philadelphia. Acting as a central government for the colonies, the congress appointed General George Washington commander in chief of the Continental Army. Washington, a Virginian, had developed a taste for battle as a young officer in the French and Indian War. "I heard the bullets whistle, and believe me, there is something charming in the sound," he wrote after surviving his first armed conflict in that war.

Washington headed for Cambridge, Massachusetts, to take command of the colonial forces surrounding Boston. On the way, he spent a night in New Haven. The next morning, he and his aide, General Charles Lee, inspected the Yale militia. As the students marched in unison, Noah Webster played "Yankee Doodle" on his flute. The generals "expressed

During the French and Indian War, British soldiers sang "Yankee Doodle" to make fun of the rustic colonists, or "Yankees," serving beside them. By the 1770s, American patriots were adopting the tune as their own. In this popular nineteenth-century print by the artist Archibald M. Willard, American musicians play the song to bolster their countrymen's fighting spirit in battle.

their surprise & gratification at the precision with which the students performed the customary exercises," Webster later recalled. The Yale militia then had the honor of escorting the generals out of town. "It fell to my humble lot to lead the company with music," Webster wrote. He remained proud of his role in the day's events for the rest of his life.

The siege of Boston dragged on through the winter. At last, on March 4, 1776, more than fifty heavy guns arrived, having been dragged through snow and over frozen rivers all the way from Fort Ticonderoga in New York. This artillery caught the British by surprise—and rather than storm the heights where Washington had positioned the guns, the British escaped Boston on ships bound for Canada.

Four months later, the Continental Congress issued the Declaration of Independence. This historic document proclaimed that the Americans were no longer British subjects, but citizens of "free and independent States." Fighting had been going on for more than a year, since the clashes at Lexington and Concord. But on July 4, 1776, when fifty-six patriots signed their names to the Declaration of Independence, the American Revolution officially began. America and Great Britain were engaged in a war to decide who would govern the British colonies in the New World: king and Parliament, or the colonists themselves.

A hundred and fifty miles away in New Haven, lectures and recitations continued at Yale until August, when typhoid broke out. Poor sanitation allowed disease-causing bacteria to travel through the water supply to all parts of the city. Typhoid was a terrifying illness. Those infected grew delirious as their fevers rose to dangerous heights. Many died from internal bleeding and acute abdominal infection. President Daggett closed the college and sent the students home until fall.

At home Noah saw his older brother, Abraham, who was living a sad, hard life. Abraham had married only to lose his wife in childbirth and watch his infant son die. Wanting to get away, he joined the Continental Army and fought as far north as Canada. His commanding officer, General Richard Montgomery, died in a failed assault on Quebec. (Joel Barlow's brother Sam also died in this battle.) Abraham Webster survived, but he was one of three hundred soldiers captured by the British. In prison he came down with smallpox, another illness colonial Americans greatly feared. It scared the British, too, so much that they turned Abraham loose. For once he was fortunate; a Frenchwoman took pity on

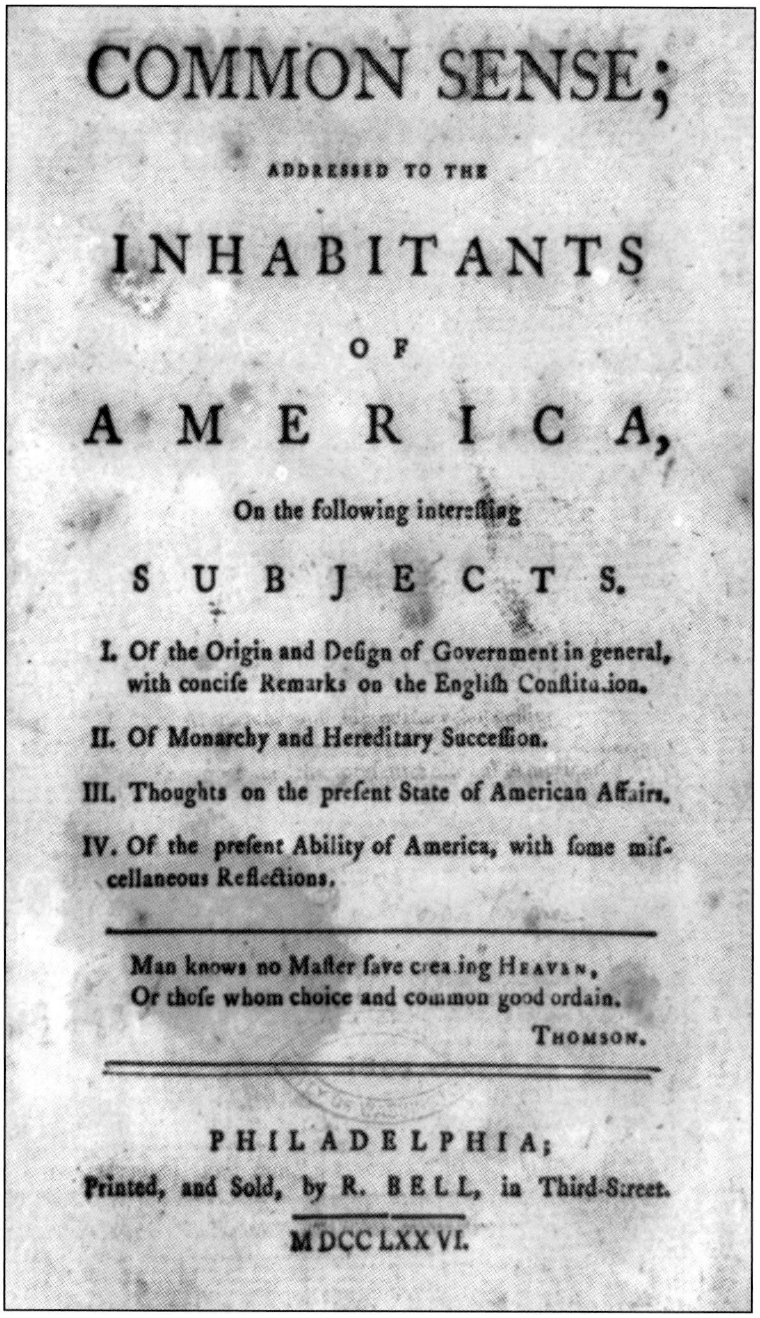

**COMMON SENSE;**

ADDRESSED TO THE

**INHABITANTS**

O F

**A M E R I C A,**

On the following interesting

**S U B J E C T S.**

I. Of the Origin and Design of Government in general, with concise Remarks on the English Constitution.

II. Of Monarchy and Hereditary Succession.

III. Thoughts on the present State of American Affairs.

IV. Of the present Ability of America, with some miscellaneous Reflections.

Man knows no Master save creating HEAVEN,
Or those whom choice and common good ordain.
THOMSON.

**PHILADELPHIA;**
Printed, and Sold, by R. BELL, in Third-Street.
MDCCLXXVI.

Thomas Paine's pamphlet *Common Sense* had ignited the fire of independence in many colonial hearts in 1776. In its pages Paine condemned the British monarchy. "Of more worth is one honest man to society, and in the sight of God, than all the crowned ruffians that ever lived," he wrote.

him. She sheltered him in her cabin and fed him milk, the only food she could spare. Abraham lived, and when he was well enough, he made his way home to Hartford.

Abraham rejoined his unit later that summer. As he rode his own horse north, Noah accompanied him on their father's horse. Noah was to then lead Abraham's mount back home. The brothers rode into New York, to an encampment beside South Bay, a finger-shaped body of water that joins Lake Champlain. There Noah greeted Ashbel Wells, a friend from Hartford who had become a soldier, and he slept that night in Wells's tent — or at least he tried. "The musketoes were so numerous that the soldiers could not sleep at night except by filling their tents with smoke," Noah noted. He spent the next night on the bay, in a flat-bottomed boat. The Webster brothers then moved on to Abraham's destination, Mount Independence, a fortress overlooking Lake Champlain. Sickness spread rapidly in soldiers' crowded quarters, and at Mount Independence the brothers saw men suffering from dysentery and fever. "The very air was infected," Noah wrote.

He returned to Yale in September to find that a big chunk of the dilapidated Old College had tumbled down. Dormitories had been lost, so the young men squeezed four to a room in other buildings. The breakdown of trade caused by war, coupled with the army's needs, meant there was never enough food or firewood. Students burned straw for warmth and came close to setting Connecticut Hall on fire. Again and again they were sent home or relocated to other towns where conditions were

An artist working in 1876 imagined the scene in Philadelphia a century earlier, when John Nixon, an American militia officer, stood on the steps of the Pennsylvania State House to read aloud the Declaration of Independence.

better. Noah's class spent a few months in Glastonbury, which was closer to Hartford than to New Haven. The constant interruptions vexed Noah, who was trying to become a learned man. On March 29, 1777, with British warships threatening New Haven, Old Tunker gave up. He shut down the college and resigned as president.

Back in the West Division, Noah's father was captain of the "alarm list," the men who formed the local militia. That September he called them to arms because the British were moving down from the north. An English general, John Burgoyne, had captured Fort Ticonderoga. He marched eight thousand soldiers to Saratoga, New York, and was pre-

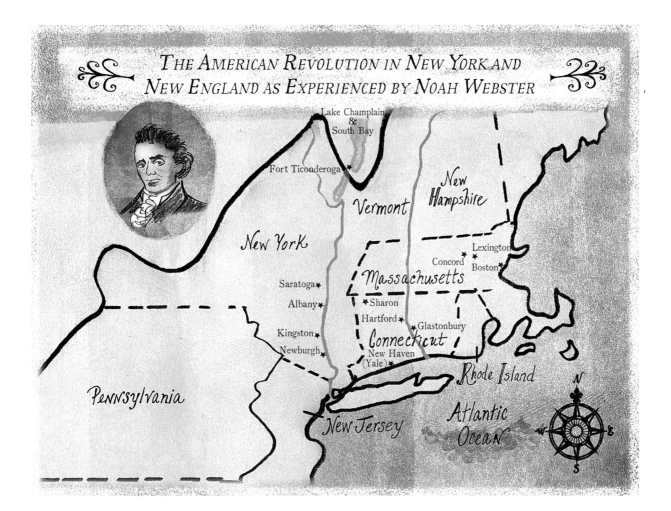

pared to move on to the city of Albany. "Terror and devastation were
spread throughout the northern counties of New York, and the adja-
cent settlements of Vermont," Webster remembered. Because all three
Webster brothers were at home, all three went along when the West Division men marched off to stop General Burgoyne, although Charles Webster was only fifteen.

Two days of marching brought them to the east bank of the Hudson
River, across from Kingston, New York, where militia companies were
amassing. The combined militias hoped to prevent Burgoyne from joining
forces with another British general, Sir Henry Clinton, who was bringing

gunboats upriver from New York City. If the generals met, then Britain would have an unbroken line of army posts stretching from Canada to Manhattan. They would cut off New England from the southern colonies and, they hoped, defeat the rebellion.

The West Division militia was marching toward Albany on October 13 when a courier rode up shouting, "Burgoyne is taken, Burgoyne is taken!" News quickly spread that the Americans had beaten Burgoyne in two battles at Saratoga. It was a decisive victory, one that showed Britain's old enemy, France, that the former colonists had a chance of winning this war. Eager to see the British defeated, the French joined the fight on the American side.

Webster would never recall this day without shedding tears of joy. "An army of British regulars had for the first time surrendered to a body of undisciplined Continental troops," he wrote. Clinton turned back, but not before firing his shipboard cannons at Kingston, then the capital of New York, and setting the town on fire.

Eight months later, Webster was back in New Haven, where Yale's ambitious new president, the Reverend Ezra Stiles, had dreams of turning the college into one of the world's great universities — someday. In 1778, in the midst of war, he felt lucky to keep Yale open. On July 23, the college held exercises for the graduating class, which included Noah Webster and Joel Barlow. The seniors had to show off all they had learned and prove they had earned their degrees. In the morning they displayed their knowledge in public examinations. In the afternoon they debated an

General John Burgoyne's surrender at Saratoga, New York, on October 17, 1777, spared the West Hartford militia from entering battle.

assigned topic: whether the destruction of the great library at Alexandria, in ancient Egypt, and the "Ignorance of the Middle Ages" were "Events unfortunate to Literature." Webster was one of the students who "disputed inimitably well," according to President Stiles.

Then the ten highest-ranking seniors spoke. When his turn came, Webster gave a speech on natural philosophy. For sixteen minutes his voice rang out over the heads of teachers and students. He told them how "nature has a peculiar happy effect." It teaches the mind "to despise the trivial foibles of custom and habit," and "to discard the inflexible attachments of bigoted superstition." Webster seemed to describe his own spirit when he proclaimed, "The human mind is naturally restless and inquisitive; its taste for curiosity, insatiable."

It was time for taking the next steps in life. Neither Noah Webster nor Joel Barlow could rely on wealth or family connections to get ahead, yet this seemed not to worry Joel. "We are not the first men in the world to have broke loose from college without fortune to puff us into public notice," he told his friend. But if there was ever a place where virtue and worthiness would lead to success, "it is in America."

# CHAPTER 3

# SEEKING A LIVING

NOT A SINGLE profession appealed to Noah Webster—not business, not law, not medicine, not teaching, and not the ministry. He wanted only to read and write. He hung around his family's house, putting off the future.

Then, one crisp fall day, his father handed him an eight-dollar bill. "You must now seek your own living," Noah Webster, Sr., said. "I can do no more for you." To the older man's way of thinking, this was true. He had gone into debt to pay for young Noah's education and had nothing left to give. As a farmer without resources, he was simply being practical.

New England was loveliest at that time of year. The leaves had turned yellow, orange, and cranberry red, making hills look like brightly printed calico. Fields of corn, wheat, and oats had been harvested, and orchards had been picked clean. The landscape awaited its first glistening frost.

Inside the clapboard farmhouse, the square-jawed youth with bright red hair fought back childish tears. He looked down at the bill in his hands. It was Continental currency, printed in Philadelphia to finance the American Revolution. It had lost value since it was issued in 1775 and was worth about two dollars in silver, a paltry sum. In that moment Noah Junior felt abandoned. "Set afloat in the world at the inexperienced age of 20, without a father's aid," he was "overwhelmed with gloomy apprehensions," he said. "I knew not what business to attempt nor by what way to obtain subsistence." His father's cold matter-of-factness stung so sharply that Noah never forgot the shock, sadness, and worry he felt upon being turned out of his home.

He sought comfort from one of his best friends, a book. *The Rambler,* by the English author Samuel Johnson, offered advice to people seeking direction in life. "The safe and general antidote against sorrow is employment," Johnson wrote, so Noah found himself a job. He returned to Glastonbury, where he had lived for a time while in college, and taught in a common school. But by winter his spirits were low again. He liked seeing his pupils learn, but he hated everything else about his life. For one thing, he had to be both teacher and custodian, cleaning the school when lessons were over, and making repairs. For another, he had to board in his pupils' homes, staying first with one family and then with another. He was never at ease; in this time of war and shortages, families shared food and warmth grudgingly. Finally, for all his hard work and inconvenience, Schoolmaster Webster earned a measly two pounds a month. (There was no standard currency during the American Revolution. The Continental

The English writer Samuel Johnson (1709–1784) is remembered for his poems, essays, and literary criticism, but is most famous for writing *A Dictionary of the English Language*. First published in 1755, Johnson's dictionary was widely used for more than a century.

Congress printed dollars, but each of the thirteen states issued money as well. Connecticut's monetary system was like Britain's, with pounds, shillings, and pence.)

Noah complained to Joel Barlow, who was also teaching school. Joel counseled his friend to have faith in a better future. Noah would make a name for himself one day—Joel was sure of it. "I have too much confidence in your merits, both as to greatness of genius and goodness of heart," he wrote. Maybe Joel was right and brighter times would come, but Noah would never get ahead teaching in Glastonbury, no matter how much genius or goodness he possessed. He left his job after the winter term to try for a career in law. Joel Barlow, meanwhile, used his Yale degree to get hired as an army chaplain.

There was no such thing as a law school in America in 1779. To become a lawyer, a young man worked alongside a practicing attorney and studied books. He then took a bar exam, and if he passed he was allowed to practice law in the state. Webster studied with Oliver Ellsworth, a respected Hartford lawyer. Ellsworth was an attorney for the State of Connecticut and a delegate to the Continental Congress.

He was also living proof that someone from a modest family could succeed. He had struggled through the first three years of his career, earning just nine Connecticut pounds from the practice of law while he also worked a small farm. One day in court, Ellsworth overheard someone say about him, "Who is that young man?—

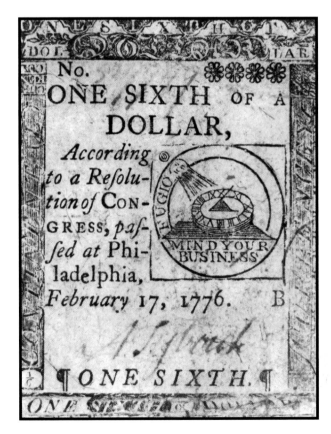

The Continental Congress issued paper money, such as this bill worth one-sixth of a dollar, to help pay the cost of fighting the American Revolution. By the war's end, this money had little or no value.

Attorney Oliver Ellsworth acted as Noah Webster's mentor when Webster was studying law. He later served as a United States senator from Connecticut and as the third chief justice of the U.S. Supreme Court.

he speaks well." These simple words changed his life. They made him feel sure of himself and inspired him to learn still more about law. By the time Webster joined him, more than a thousand cases awaited Ellsworth's attention.

Webster stayed in Ellsworth's home, but he still needed to make money while he learned, so he taught at the Brick School House, a nearby private school. Webster drove himself hard. He taught all day long from

Monday through Friday and for half a day on Saturday. In the remaining hours he assisted Ellsworth in his legal practice. Then, when all his other work was done, he studied late into the night in Ellsworth's large library.

It was all too much. Noah grew so exhausted that he fell ill and had to return to his family's farmhouse to rest. But living at home free of charge was out of the question, since his father had insisted he earn his own way. As soon as he was well enough, Noah started teaching at the school he had attended as a boy and paying his parents room and board. That winter he trudged four miles to work through snowdrifts high enough to bury fences.

In summer 1780 he had a chance to study law again while working for a judge in the large town of Litchfield. Judge Jedediah Strong was also Litchfield's recorder of deeds. He was described as a small man with a "limping gait, and an unpleasant countenance," but what he lacked in looks he made up for in skill. His knowledge of legal forms and his clear handwriting brought him many clients. Strong had lost his wife and was raising a small daughter. As Noah helped Strong keep track of documents relating to land ownership, the judge taught him about matters of law. Noah also attended lectures at the home of Tapping Reeve, a leading Litchfield lawyer who in a few years would found one of the first law schools in the United States. When he had time, Noah visited his married sister Jerusha, who lived nearby.

Noah Webster prepared himself well, and on an evening in March 1781, he presented himself at the Litchfield courthouse to be examined for admission to the bar. Some twenty candidates took the test, but not a single one passed. Noah was sure the results were rigged, that county officials thought twenty new lawyers were twenty too many and so failed them all. He went home to Hartford and took another bar exam, and this time he passed. He found no work as a lawyer, though. "The practice of law," he wrote, "was in good measure set aside by the general calamity." This was true. Many people had decided that legal matters could wait until peace returned and the economy improved.

Webster had no choice but to fall back on his other profession, teaching. Instead of becoming a town schoolmaster, this time he opened his own school. He moved to the woodsy village of Sharon, in northeastern Connecticut. He boarded in the home of a clergyman, Parson Cotton Smith, and conducted his school in the attic of Smith's big stone house. "Young Gentlemen and Ladies may be instructed in Reading, Writing, Mathematicks, the English Language, and if desired, the Latin and Greek Languages — in Geography, Vocal Music, &c.," stated Webster's advertisement in the *Connecticut Courant.*

The subjects taught at this private school went far beyond what children learned in a town's common school. And Webster offered girls the same course of study as boys, which was rare in early America. Boys from families that could afford private schooling generally studied subjects such as Latin, Greek, and geometry. Girls, meanwhile, were tutored in pretty pastimes: needlework, drawing, music, and the like. Webster may have been ahead of his time in instructing girls, but he stopped short of calling men and women equals. "That education is always *wrong,* which raises a woman above the duties of her station," he claimed. By "her station" he meant her role in the family. "In America, female education should have for its object what is *useful*"; that is, what is useful for a mother instructing her children and a wife serving as her husband's worthy companion.

Webster opened his school at exactly the right time. Many well-to-do patriots had fled New York City when it fell to the British in October 1776. They sought safety in the countryside, in places like Sharon. They were looking for schools for their children, who had been uprooted as well.

The months Webster spent in Sharon were happy ones. He shared his love of music by leading a singing school for young gentlemen and ladies. He liked being part of Parson Smith's cultured household. John Cotton Smith, age thirteen, was preparing to enter Yale. His smart twenty-year-old sister, Juliana, edited the magazine of the Sharon Literary Club. At weekly meetings the club members read their own writing aloud and practiced debating. Afterward they enjoyed refreshments and sometimes danced. Writing, reading, debating, and dancing: the Sharon Literary Club seemed to be planned with Noah Webster in mind. He was an enthusiastic member.

At one meeting, he read an essay he wrote on a moral subject. This piece of writing has been lost, but Juliana Smith's scathing comments have survived the passage of time. Juliana confided to her brother that

Webster's "reflections are as prosy as those of our horse." What was worse, "in conversation, he is even duller than in writing, if that be possible." Yet, she noted, "He is a painstaking man and a hard student. Papa says he will make his mark."

Webster was indeed a very hard student. In fall 1781, he returned to Yale to receive his master's degree. To do this he wrote a scholarly paper, or dissertation, and gave a speech on his chosen topic during the commencement. September 12 was a joyful day in New Haven as Yale held its first commencement in seven years. The war was winding down, and it was safe enough for crowds to gather on campus again. Webster spoke about education and religion, and how they went hand in hand. Throughout history, "improvement of the human mind" aided the spread of religion, he said.

While at Yale, Webster saw Joel Barlow, who was also receiving a master's degree that day. For his dissertation, Barlow read sections of a long poem he was composing, *The Vision of Columbus*. In this poem Barlow imagined Christopher Columbus looking into the future to see an American nation on which "all the majesty of nature smiles":

> *Bays stretch their arms and mountains lift the skies;*
> *The lakes, unfolding, point the streams their way,*
> *The plains, the hills their lengthening skirts display . . .*

The nation Barlow praised still lacked a central government. In March

1781, the Continental Congress had voted to accept the Articles of Confederation, a document that laid the foundation for a government with limited power. This government was to have no leader and no national courts. Its congress could pass laws, but it had no way to make the states enforce them. It could not raise taxes, so it depended on the states for money. The arrangement pleased those Americans who considered the state where they lived to be their true country. They wanted the union to be nothing more than a "firm league of friendship" among the states.

Meanwhile, many people in Great Britain had become fed up with the American Revolution, which felt to them like a long, distant war. It seemed to General George Washington that one more British loss like the one at Saratoga might convince the enemy to surrender. His chance came when the English general Charles Cornwallis moved his army into Virginia and set up camp at Portsmouth, at the entrance to the Chesapeake Bay. As Continental infantry forces bombarded Cornwallis's men on land, French naval vessels blocked the Chesapeake, preventing British ships from getting through with aid.

The British general Charles Cornwallis offers his sword to the American commander, George Washington, in a gesture of surrender on October 19, 1781.

Cornwallis was forced to surrender on October 19, ending the last great battle of the war.

After Britain's Parliament voted to give up the fight on March 4, 1782, displaced New Yorkers left towns like Sharon and went home. Noah Webster lost most of his students, so he closed his school. Having saved enough of his earnings to support himself for several months, he devoted the winter to the things he loved most: his books and his pen.

He was pondering the future of his new nation. If Americans were to govern themselves, then people from all walks of life had to know how to read and write. All Americans should be able to add and subtract, and have some knowledge of history and geography, Webster believed. Farmers and shopkeepers needed schooling as much as state and national leaders did. If education belonged only to the wealthy and privileged, then a class of aristocrats would arise and take power, as had happened in Europe.

He also dwelled on current events. The American Revolution had been won. Yet even as representatives of the United States and Great Britain were working out a treaty in Paris, some Americans were calling for a return to British rule. They included Silas Deane, who had represented Connecticut in the Continental Congress. Deane questioned whether Americans were more secure under democracy than they were before the Revolution began. He asked, "Will our commerce flourish more under independency, than it did whilst we were connected to Great Britain?" Deane thought not. He foresaw that "the jarring interests of the different States, will be such . . . that we shall be happy even to escape for any time the going into a civil war among ourselves."

The notion that Americans should give up their hard-won independence infuriated Webster. He penned a long, impassioned article, "Observations on the Revolution of America," which appeared in the *New-York Packet,* a weekly newspaper. If readers would only recall the events of the past twenty years, he wrote, they would understand why reverting to British rule was a bad idea. "The perpetual opposition of the Americans to acts of the British parliament; the open quarrels and insurrections, occasioned by their attempts to enforce those acts, some of which proceeded to bloodshed, are proof sufficient that a dependence on foreign government is incompatible with the tranquility of America."

Independent America would be a shining example for the rest of the world, Webster predicted. "The unlimited advantage of freedom . . . enjoyed no where but in America, must in time, have considerable influence in unfettering the shackles which are so generally rivetted upon the human race."

In spring 1782, Noah Webster left Sharon. He never said why, but according to local gossip, he was disappointed in love. He had been courting a local beauty, the story goes, and may have proposed marriage, but she dropped him when an earlier suitor came home from the war. Noah may also have been spurned by Juliana Smith, who found him so hopelessly dull.

Webster moved to Goshen, New York, a village forty miles to the west. Goshen was home to the notorious "hanging tree," where Claudius

At the close of the American Revolution, General George Washington maintained his headquarters at Newburgh, New York, overlooking the Hudson River.

Smith, "the cowboy of the Ramapos," was executed in January 1779. Smith and his band of guerrilla fighters had robbed and terrorized the families of the Ramapo Mountains of New Jersey and New York during the recent war, and had murdered an army officer. With the coming of peace, life was returning to normal in Goshen, and the community needed teachers.

To reach Goshen, Webster crossed the Hudson River by ferry and came ashore at Newburgh, New York, the site of General Washington's headquarters. He saw the Continental Army assembled there in camps, waiting to be disbanded. Wandering among the soldiers' huts of timber and stone, he was startled to hear a raucous jangle of words. Many men from Pennsylvania spoke German, while some New Yorkers chatted in Dutch. Webster heard fragments of conversations in French and in the Gaelic tongues of Ireland and Scotland. Yet all the speakers were Americans. They were using the languages they spoke at home and in which they might even have been schooled.

The men speaking English were often just as hard to understand. Webster struggled to make sense of the English spoken by soldiers from the Deep South or the wilds of northern New Hampshire. "Every State in America and almost every town in each State, has some peculiarities in pronunciation which are equally erroneous," he observed. Southerners said "saft" instead of "soft," and "resins" when they meant "raisins." Awful! Some New Englanders spoke with "a flat drawling pronunciation." Deplorable!

The United States would never succeed with such a mishmash of languages, and Noah Webster was not the only one who thought so. Many people agreed that the nation needed a single tongue, but they argued about what it should be. Most Americans spoke English, but English was the language of the enemy. Some called for the adoption of German, or even a classical language such as Hebrew. Others had no objection to speaking English as long as they called it something else—perhaps Columbian. "Let us make it as familiar to our ears to say that a foreigner speaks good *Columbian* as it is to say that he speaks good *English,*" proposed one American. Webster thought Americans should speak English, and he was happy to call it English. But it had to be an American form of English, one suited to American life.

# CHAPTER 4

# A New Book to Teach a New Nation

NOAH WEBSTER arrived in Goshen possessing seventy-five cents and knowing not a soul. He swept the dust from a private school that had closed during the war, and opened it for students. He wisely took payment in silver dollars, which held their value better than paper money did. Although his pockets filled, he fell into "extreme depression," he wrote. He spent lonely days and nights full of "gloomy forebodings."

The tricky subject of Americans' speech bothered his mind. If the jumble of languages spoken in the United States posed a problem, then the nation's schoolmasters were a big part of it, he concluded. Most had too little training to teach children correctly. Even worse, "The principal part of instructors are illiterate people," Webster declared. To help young Americans speak properly, teachers needed "some easy guide to the *standard* of pronunciation."

No easy guide existed, though. The book most people relied on was

*A New Guide to the English Tongue,* the text Webster had studied as a child in school. But the grown-up Webster found fault with Thomas Dilworth's book. To Webster, the way Dilworth divided words into syllables was all wrong. Wherever possible, Dilworth made each syllable start with a consonant, regardless of how the word was pronounced. He broke *many* into syllables as *ma ny,* for example, and he divided *level* as *le vel.* It was much more helpful to divide these words in a way that showed how people said them, Webster thought: *man y; lev el.* The short sound of the first vowel would be clearer this way; students would know not to say "mayny" or "leevel." Dilworth's treatment of words that ended in *tion* and *sion* also drove Webster crazy. Anyone learning to speak from Dilworth's book would think *nation* had three syllables: *na ti on.*

Just as dreadful was Dilworth's list of proper nouns. Webster counted too many names of places in England and saw that America was ignored. Dilworth also mentioned God too often, to Webster's way of thinking. Webster saw nothing wrong with teaching religion in school, but it had to be given in the proper dose. "Nothing has a greater tendency to lessen the reverence which mankind ought to have for the Supreme Being," he wrote, "than a careless repetition of his name upon every trifling occasion." Finally, when it came to Dilworth's grammar, well, Webster was not impressed: "One half of the work is totally useless and the other half defective and erroneous."

If Webster wanted a book for teaching American English to the American people, then he had to write it himself. Certain that "the spelling book does more to form the language of a nation than all other books,"

| 40 | *A* N E W G U I D E | | |
|---|---|---|---|
| fat ten | fro"fty | hea"vy | lu ftre |
| fau cet | fruit ful | heed lefs | Ma dam |
| faul ty | fru"ftrate | heir efs | ma'gic |
| fear lefs | Gain ful | high way | ma'lice |
| fea"ther | ga"ther | hi"gler | man'gle |
| fea ture | gau dy | hi"ther | ma'fter |
| fe"fter | ge"fture | ho"mage | ma'ftiff |
| fierce ly | ghoft ly | ho'neft | match lefs |
| fifth ly | gi"blets | hoft efs | mea zles |
| fla gon | giv er | hour ly | me'lon |
| flam beau | giv en | hum ble | me'rit |
| fla vour | gloo my | hun'ger | me'thod |
| flax en | good nefs | hun'gry | migh ty |
| fol low | go"vern | I'mage | mif chief |
| fon dle | grace lefs | in fight | mi ftrefs |
| foot pace | grand fon | Jew el | mo'dern |
| foot pad | gra"vel | jour nal | mo'deft |
| foot ftep | grea fy | juice lefs | mon ftrous |
| fo"reign | great nefs | jui cy | mo'ther |
| forethought | griev ous | Kind nefs | moun tain |
| for trefs | grift ly | kna vifh | mourn ful |
| found er | gro"gram | knighthood | muf'cle |
| fourth ly | ground lefs | knock er | mu'fket |
| frail ty | grum ble | know ledge | mu'flin |
| frec kle | gui"nea | knuc kle | mu'ftard |
| freck led | Ha"bit | Lan'guage | mu'fter |
| freck ly | haf-fock | lau rel | mu'fty |
| free ly | ha vock | lea'ther | Name lefs |
| free ftone | haut boy | le'vel | naugh ty |
| friend lefs | heal thy | light er | need ful |
| fright en | heart en | li'mit | neigh bour |
| fright ful | heart lefs | li'quor | nei ther |
| fro"lic | hea then | lu cre | ne'ver |
| | | | nofe gay |

Dilworth offered pupils lists of words divided into syllables. Webster thought his way of dividing words was flawed. It was also inconsistent, as can be seen by the divisions of *freckle* and *freckled.*

he rolled up his sleeves and got busy. As he wrote, his depression dissolved.

Most teachers in Webster's day believed that learning to spell was the first step in learning to read, even though the rules of spelling were still fairly new. Two centuries earlier, in the 1500s, there was no right or wrong way to spell a word. Each person decided how best to express the sound of a word with letters. *Tung, plainlie, appeer, fascion, woord*—one Englishman came up with these spellings when writing a letter in 1561. Some authors spelled the same word several different ways within a single book: *fellow, felow, felowe, fallow, fallowe.* All this creative spelling caused confusion.

Thinking that a standard system would help, a number of people proposed solutions. Some put forth ideas that hardly anyone seemed to like, such as adding more letters to the alphabet. Others made suggestions that caught on, such as doing away with double consonants at the ends of many words. Everyone could see that it was simpler to write *put* than *putt,* or *led* than *ledd.* By 1650 or so, rules for spelling had taken hold.

When writing his book, Webster saw no need to start from scratch. He worked from Dilworth's text, keeping the parts he liked and tossing out those that vexed him. He divided words into syllables using his own system, and he grouped words according to how they sounded rather than how they were spelled. How else, he asked, "would a child or a foreigner learn the different sounds of *o* in these words, *rove, move, dove?*" In Webster's book, rhyming words like *be, flea,* and *key* belonged together, even though their spellings differed.

The list of places in Webster's speller included the thirteen states, their capitals, and other American cities and towns. At the end of the book he added "A Chronological Account of Remarkable Events in America," which was a timeline spanning from 1492 and Columbus's first voyage through the end of the Revolutionary War. Teaching American history in school was something new, but Webster was sure that knowing their common heritage would help unite the nation's children. In place of Dilworth's religious teachings, Webster added sage advice such as this: "Be not wise in thine own eyes; but be humble. Let truth only proceed from thy mouth."

Webster tested his ideas in his own school. To his great joy, he discovered that his lists of rhyming words helped the children learn to read. Webster was a zealous teacher who hoped his love of learning would rub off on his pupils. As soon as they could read well enough, he handed them writings by great Americans, from George Washington to Thomas Paine.

Noah Webster planned to call his spelling book *The American Instructor.* He dreamed of seeing it in print, but he faced huge hurdles. For one thing, he was too poor to pay for the printing. For another, even if he managed to get his book published, he would be competing against Dilworth. Used in schools throughout the United States, the Englishman's book was everywhere. Truly, as Joel Barlow said, "old Dilworth" was "the nurse of us all."

There was yet another barrier to publication, and it was a big one: the United States had no copyright law. A copyright blocks other people from stealing an author's work or publishing it without permission. With no copyright protection, anyone could take credit for an author's writing, keep the profit earned from selling it, and still be acting within the law. In fact, this kind of piracy happened all the time in the young nation. Even Webster himself felt no shame about copying parts of Dilworth's book. Britain's copyright law had covered works published in the colonies before the Revolutionary War, but British laws no longer applied in the United States.

In August 1782, Noah Webster did what he saw as the only logical thing. He packed up his manuscript and went to Philadelphia. He planned to appear in person and persuade Congress to pass the needed law. Making an overland journey was no easy feat in the young United States, whether a traveler took a coach, rode a horse, or walked. People traversing the unpaved roads in dry weather were covered in dust, and mud slowed them down when it was wet. An unexpected stump or rut might turn a carriage over, and a fallen tree might halt progress altogether.

Webster was lucky and reached Philadelphia without much trouble. Once there, he spent each day outside the two-story brick building known as Independence Hall, where the Continental Congress met, hoping to

A coach sets off on a muddy, rutted road in this early American illustration. Travel presented challenges in the eighteenth century, regardless of the mode of transportation chosen.

catch the ears of gentlemen of influence. In the evening, in taverns and inns, he told his story to James Madison of Virginia and other delegates. The boyish Madison avoided the many "impertinent fops" who sought his attention, but this earnest teacher from New York was saying something worth hearing. Madison agreed with Webster that the United States needed a copyright law, but he said the Continental Congress could do nothing to help. Under the Articles of Confederation, the Congress had no power to enact or enforce this kind of legislation. If the United States was going to have copyright laws, then they had to come from each of the states.

So Webster did the next logical thing. He took his argument to the states. Pennsylvania's state legislators were home on recess, so he headed for Trenton, New Jersey, to try his luck there. He met with the governor, William Livingston, whose cousin lived in Goshen and sent his children to Webster's school. Livingston promised to introduce a copyright bill when the legislators returned from their summer vacation.

Webster then moved on to his home state, Connecticut. He stopped in at Yale and showed his manuscript to the college president, Ezra Stiles. He waited and watched as the older man turned the pages, running his eyes down Webster's sentences and lists of words. At last Stiles sat back and pronounced his judgment. He praised the content of Webster's book, but he suggested one change. Webster's title, *The American Instructor*, had to go, he said. This book needed a title that sounded important. He thought for a moment and came up with one: *A Grammatical Institute of the English Language.*

Philadelphia in 1782 was both a busy port and the meeting place of the Second Continental Congress.

What could Webster say? He liked his old title; it was easy to remember, and it contained the word *American*. He hated Stiles's version, which was lofty and long. Yet he needed men like Ezra Stiles on his side. If he ever managed to publish his book, an endorsement from the president of Yale College might persuade some town fathers to use it in their schools. So Webster swallowed his disappointment and tried to like Stiles's title.

He went on to the capital city of Hartford, where he asked the state assembly to pass a law that would grant him the exclusive right of "printing, publishing & vending" his book in Connecticut. This petition marked the first time anyone tried formally to get a copyright law passed in the United States. The assembly acted slowly, so Webster could only wait and worry. Would he ever publish his book? He also wrestled with a larger question: Would the nation survive under the Articles of Confederation? He had been to Philadelphia and had seen for himself that Congress was powerless to act.

Webster saw his family before leaving Hartford, and picked up his brother Charles. Although Charles was twenty years old and grown up, he was going to enroll in Noah's school. By teaching his younger brother free of charge, Noah hoped to pay

The Reverend Ezra Stiles, president of Yale College from 1778 until 1795, advised Webster to call his spelling book *A Grammatical Institute of the English Language.* Webster hated the title.

back some of the money his father had spent to send him to Yale. Noah Senior wished his sons well. "I rejoyce to hear that there is a prospect of your doing good and benefiting yourselves," he told them. "I wish to have you serve your generation and do good in the world and be useful."

Noah Webster labored without rest through the fall and winter, teaching school and polishing his manuscript. Again he drove himself to exhaustion. By year's end he found it impossible to have two jobs, teacher and author. He closed his school, although it meant letting his brother down, and on January 6, a downcast Charles started for home.

He stopped off in Sharon to deliver a letter from Noah to John Canfield, a Connecticut assemblyman who lived in the town.

The young teacher had written movingly about his work. "However some may think a book of this kind too trifling for public notice, I am fully of the opinion that the reformation of the language we speak will some time or other be thought an object of legislative importance," read the letter. Webster was sure that his plain little book could reach rich and poor, city dwellers and country folk alike. It was "like a star," he wrote, which "casts its beams equally upon the peasant and the monarch." If only it could be copyrighted!

Canfield was persuaded. Off he went to Hartford, where he spoke to his fellow assemblymen, making the case for a copyright law. Meanwhile, an author named John Ledyard came before the assembly as well. Ledyard had written an account of the final voyage of Captain James Cook that he wanted to get into print, but he needed copyright protection too. The assemblymen listened, and on January 8, 1783, they passed the nation's first copyright law. In Connecticut, authors owned the rights to their work for fourteen years from the date of publication.

Thrilled by his triumph in Connecticut, Webster campaigned for copyright laws in other states. He wrote letter after letter, appealing to anyone he could think of for help. He wrote to prominent people whose children he had taught and to powerful men throughout the country, whether he knew them or not. Gradually his effort paid off. Massachusetts enacted a copyright law on March 17, and Maryland was next, on April 21. The Continental Congress also got involved. On May 2 the

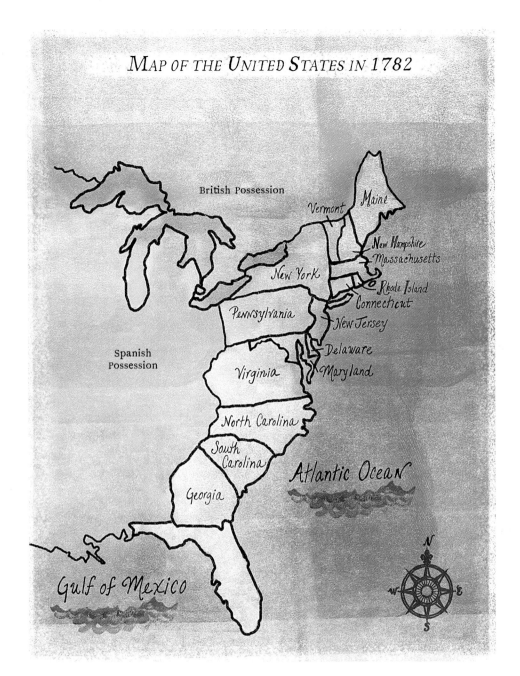

MAP OF THE UNITED STATES IN 1782

British Possession

Vermont

Maine

New Hampshire

Massachusetts

New York

Rhode Island

Connecticut

Pennsylvania

New Jersey

Spanish Possession

Delaware

Maryland

Virginia

North Carolina

South Carolina

Atlantic Ocean

Georgia

Gulf of Mexico

The number of states and their boundaries evolved between 1775, when the Americans declared their independence from Britain, and 1959, when Alaska and Hawaii were granted statehood. In 1782 both New York and New Hampshire claimed Vermont, which became a state in 1791. Maine was part of Massachusetts until it was admitted to the union as a separate state in 1820.

delegates formally recommended that the states adopt laws to protect "new books, not hitherto printed." By the end of the year, New

Jersey, New Hampshire, and Rhode Island also had the needed legislation.

As soon as Connecticut's law was on the books, Webster went to Hartford to find a publisher for his speller. He took his manuscript to print shops and showed it to the owners. One person after another praised his book; some even called it visionary. But "no printer or bookseller was found to undertake the publication at his own risk," Webster noted. There would be paper and other supplies to buy, typesetters to pay, and no promise of a profit. Some agreed to print the book if the author covered the cost. But Webster was "destitute of the means of defraying the expenses," he sadly reported.

It was a trying time, yet "his fortitude never forsook him," Webster wrote about himself, and neither did his friends. Joel Barlow offered to lend him five hundred dollars, a very large sum. Barlow's "generosity far exceeded his ability," Webster worried. He believed so strongly in his book that he took the money, although Barlow was newly married and seeking a steady line of work. (With the war over, the army no longer needed him as a chaplain.) Oliver Wolcott, Jr., another Yale classmate, also loaned Webster some money, and so did John Trumbull, the poet who taught at Yale during Webster's years there. Trumbull had left the college to become a thriving lawyer. He invited Webster to stay in his Hartford home while the pages of his book rolled off the press. The firm of Hudson and Goodwin, publisher of the *Connecticut Courant,* was to print the speller.

In August 1783, Webster's book was ready to be sold. A small volume printed on cheap paper, it was titled *A Grammatical Institute of the English Language,* Part 1, because the author was planning two more parts. The *Grammatical Institute* was going to include a grammar book and a reader as well.

Eager to let people know that his book had entered the world, Webster placed an ad in the *Connecticut Courant.* Together the three parts of the *Grammatical Institute* would offer "an easy, concise and systematic Method of EDUCATION," he boasted. A few weeks later, the paper ran a long piece by Webster in which he blatantly listed the faults in Thomas Dilworth's popular book. When it came to the pronunciation of vowels, he claimed, "The celebrated Spelling-Book of Mr. Dilworth is totally defective or erroneous." He compared Dilworth's grammar to "a scarecrow that so frightens children when they are young, that they are afraid of grammars all their lives." His own book remedied these flaws. Whether he succeeded was for "the public to examine and decide for themselves."

One person who examined Webster's book hated it. In June 1784, a Hartford newspaper printed an irate letter from a reader, complaining

The English schoolbook author Thomas Dilworth died in 1780; the anonymous critic who called himself Dilworth's Ghost had fun at Webster's expense. He pretended to be Dilworth addressing Webster from beyond the grave.

that Webster had copied most of his work from Dilworth and other authors. The angry writer signed himself "Dilworth's Ghost."

Over the next few months a flurry of letters between this anonymous writer and Noah Webster appeared in the press. Webster defended himself, responding, "Every grammar that was ever written is a compilation." The Ghost shot back that even Webster's way of dividing words into syllables was someone else's idea. This was a lie, "a bare-faced assertion!" Webster objected. Well, then, choosing such a long title, *A Grammatical Institute of the English Language,* was just plain arrogance, wrote the Ghost. The title was someone else's idea, Webster explained. The *Grammatical Institute* "was christened by the gentleman who presides over literature in Connecticut." He was referring of course to Ezra Stiles, the president of Yale.

The Ghost accused him of being proud, but Webster believed he was right to be proud. "I have too much pride not to wish to see America assume a national character. I have too much pride to stand indebted to Great Britain for books to learn our children the letters of the alphabet," he wrote. The attacks from Dilworth's Ghost annoyed him less than he let on. If they got people thinking about the *Grammatical Institute,* then maybe more customers would buy it.

Webster's pen flew across one page and then another as he wrote ads to publicize his book and letters to defend it. He also sounded off in the press on an issue that had Americans up in arms. It had to do with the government's plan to reward officers in the Continental Army.

Back in 1779, when its money was worth almost nothing, the Continental Congress had made the officers a promise. If they would keep fighting without being properly paid, they would receive a bonus later on. It would be a lump sum equaling five years' military pay. With the war over, the government wanted to keep this promise, but there was too little money in the treasury. So Congress voted to collect a tax—an *impost*—from the states.

The impost could only be levied if all the states agreed to it, but no one knew if this would happen. Many people asked why the bonus should go only to officers, and they had a good point. Ordinary soldiers had fought hard too, and they were just as deserving. Rewarding officers seemed to go against the American ideal of equality. The impost was "calculated to raise and exalt some Citizens in wealth and grandeur, to the injury and oppression of others," protested the Massachusetts legislature. At gatherings throughout Connecticut, red-faced townspeople shouted their objections. "Congress and the bold patriots of this state were represented as Tyrants," Webster wrote in his diary, "and the people as in danger of slavery."

Webster saw that something larger than the impost was at stake. It was a point that many people missed. The states needed to back the decisions of Congress—decisions made by their own representatives—if the nation was to function. With thirteen separate states calling the shots, the young republic would soon fall apart. Even if people hated the impost, the states had to endorse it for the good of the country. Alarming too was an upcoming convention in Middletown, Connecticut. Town leaders from all parts of the state planned to gather in Middletown to try to defeat the impost on their own.

Webster feared that if the citizens seized for themselves a power that belonged to the state government, anarchy would result. He sounded an alarm in the *Connecticut Courant*. "When people . . . have delegated to representatives a power to make certain laws," he bellowed, "it is treason not to obey them." Concerning a law — any law, "no matter whether it be right or wrong; in either case it ought to be strictly obeyed, so long as it is a law." He also said, "A refusal to comply with it annihilates our existence as a united body."

The people of Connecticut paid attention to these warnings. When the Middletown Convention came to order on September 8, 1783, so many people stayed away that the proceedings were postponed until September 30. The delay gave everyone time to think further about what Webster had written. When the convention gathered again, it "ended in smoke," Webster observed; it accomplished nothing. On May 19, 1784, he watched the vote in the state house as Connecticut became the final state to support the impost. He jotted triumphantly in his journal, "A happy event!"

# CHAPTER 5

# *LONELY TRAVELER*

B Y WINTER, customers had snatched up all five thousand copies of Webster's speller. So many towns wanted to use it in their schools that it was reprinted to meet the demand. In March 1784, Part 2 of the *Grammatical Institute,* the grammar book, was ready for sale.

Clearly, Connecticut liked the new spelling book, but its author wanted other states to adopt it as well. So in June 1784, he packed up as many copies as he could carry, climbed onto a horse, and rode east. He spent a month traveling in New England, promoting his work. In Providence and Newport, Rhode Island, and Springfield and Boston, Massachusetts, he gave samples to teachers and ministers. He placed ads in local newspapers, describing the wonders of his new texts for teaching American English. In each place he walked the length of every street, counting the houses. Providence had 560, according to Webster's tally; Boston, a much larger city, had 2,200.

Webster made deals with local publishers to print and sell his books in states with copyright laws. With brisk sales in Connecticut, he did not need to pay for these printings; the publishers agreed to pay him. He could have asked for a royalty, a percentage of the profit on each book sold. If a publisher sold many copies, then the author would earn a tidy sum. But Webster needed money right then and there, so rather than wait for royalties to roll in, he sold publishers the rights to his book for a flat fee. He made only a few hundred dollars, but at least he had cash in hand. Over the next few years, the publishers would sell hundreds of thousands of copies of the *Grammatical Institute,* despite its awkward title, and reap huge profits. "Could I have kept my copyright in my own hands till this time," Webster later concluded with regret, "I might now have rid in a chariot."

He made his way north to Portsmouth, New Hampshire, where he counted 450 houses and danced at a ball. "Had a fine Partner," he wrote in his diary, "but she is engaged." This was just one in a string of romantic disappointments for Noah, who was twenty-five and eager to fall in love. He met plenty of eligible women. In fact, he felt his heart "pulled twenty ways at once," he said. "The greatest difficulty, however, is that after a man has made *his* choice, it remains for the Lady to make *hers.*" And none of the ladies chose him. His fondest gaze, his sprightliest dance step, and his talk of spelling failed to impress.

Still, he went to dances in Hartford, each time with new hope. He attended a dinner honoring the Marquis de Lafayette, the French noble-man who had served as a general in the Continental Army. He was pleased

In the 1780s Boston was called the "capital of New England."

enough with himself to write in his diary on his twenty-sixth birthday, "I have lived long enough to be good and of some importance."

He joined the "Connecticut Wits," a clever group that also included Joel Barlow and John Trumbull. The Connecticut Wits were Federalists, believers in a strong central government, and feared the Articles of Confederation were leading the country toward anarchy. Some of them put their heads together to write political poems for local newspapers. These lines are from a very long poem by several Connecticut Wits called *The Anarchiad*:

> *The dreams of congress fade,*
> *The federal union sinks in endless shade,*
> *Each feeble call, that warns the realms around,*
> *Seems the faint echo of a dying sound . . .*

Noah Webster was never much of a poet, so he wrote four essays presenting his ideas on governance. In them he advised his fellow Americans to reject the notion that a central government would vie for power with the states. "Let every state reserve its sovereign right of directing its own internal affairs; but give to Congress the sole right of conducting the general affairs of the continent," he proposed. He invited his readers to think of a national government as "the general voice of the people." He wrote, "All power is vested in the people. . . . The right of making laws for the United States should be vested in all their inhabitants by legal and equal representation." If the United States was going to rise to greatness, then it needed a strong federal government, just as it needed a common language. Webster was sure of it. He also called for a national system of education and for the abolition of slavery. In 1785 he issued his essays in a pamphlet titled *Sketches of American Policy.*

That same year he also published Part 3 of the *Grammatical Institute,* the reader. He chose passages for this volume with great care. He wanted to open the world of literature to children, to help them gain "a complete knowledge of words and of the modern manner of writing." He offered selections from works by the wise Samuel Johnson, as well as from American authors such as George Washington, Benjamin Franklin, Thomas Paine, and Joel Barlow. To get young readers thinking, he inserted part of a long letter published in London by a writer named Thomas Day. In this letter Day spoke out against slavery, which he called an "attack upon the safety and happiness of our fellow creatures . . . that boldly strikes at the foundation of all humanity and justice."

Webster wrote some of the passages himself, including one titled "Character of Juliana." He described a model of young womanhood, a girl whose charms included "regular features, a fine complexion . . . and those blushes of modesty that soften the soul of the beholder." People may admire her beauty, Webster wrote, but when they "hear the melting expressions of unaffected sensibility and virtue that flow from her tongue, her personal charms receive new lustre, and irresistibly engage the affections of her acquaintances." Was this passage about Juliana Smith of Sharon? Did Webster still care for her?

He was living in the home of a Hartford physician and handling a few legal cases. But with his books finished, he needed more to do. He was drifting through bland days, neither "plunged in calamities nor overwhelmed with the blessings of heaven," he noted, and he was restless. He thought about all the children to the south. If only these children could learn to speak and read English from the *Grammatical Institute*! In May 1785, he embarked on a trip that would keep him away from home for more than a year. He set out to introduce the South to his schoolbooks and lobby for copyright laws in states that still lacked them. Before leaving he sent a supply of his books to the growing city of Baltimore, which would be his home base for the next six months.

Its location on the Chesapeake Bay in Maryland made Baltimore the ideal port for shipping grain from local farms to distant markets. With three hundred houses being built each year and streets needing to be paved with cobblestones, noisy Baltimore offered jobs aplenty to immigrants willing to work. "The spirit of building exceeds belief," remarked

General Nathaniel Greene, a hero of the Revolution who passed through town in 1783, and he was right. When Noah Webster arrived, Baltimore was fast becoming the fourth-largest city in the United States. He counted 1,950 houses there.

Almost as soon as he settled himself in a lodging house, Webster hired a horse and rode fifty miles to Mount Vernon, George Washington's Virginia estate. After giving Washington a letter of introduction from John Trumbull, Webster shook hands with the famous general, who had retired after the war and become a gentleman farmer. Webster had seen the great man once before, when Washington passed through New Haven in 1775, but had never met him until this moment.

Washington invited Webster to stay for dinner, which was served promptly at three o'clock. There were pancakes for dessert, but Webster refused the molasses that he was offered to pour on them. His excuse, that as a New Englander he had already eaten too much molasses, struck Washington as funny. "The General burst out with a loud laugh, a thing unusual with him," Webster noted. Washington laughed not because molasses was a key ingredient in baked beans or Injun pudding, both popular New England dishes, but because he was reminded of something that had happened during the Revolution. When a wagon turned over, causing a barrel of molasses to break open, soldiers rushed to fill their hats with the sticky syrup, saving what they could.

Webster gave Washington a copy of *Sketches of American Policy,* and the two men discussed issues that faced their new nation: whether the United States should have a strong central government, if slavery would persist, and the likelihood of having a national system of education. In the evening Martha Washington joined the gentlemen for whist, a popular card game, and Webster found the general's wife to be "very social." He spent the night at Mount Vernon and rode back to Baltimore the next day.

A short time later he boarded a ship called the *George,* which was bound for Charleston, South Carolina. Two days of sailing brought the vessel to its first stop, Norfolk, Virginia, where Webster stretched his legs on land. During the Revolution, Norfolk was burned to the ground by the British navy, which bombarded the shoreline with its big guns, and by Continental forces, which destroyed the houses and shops of people loyal to the Crown. Webster reckoned that "two or three hundred houses well built of brick" lined the streets, but the town still bore the scars of war and had "not recovered its former elegance," he wrote. A bountiful early crop of peas had sprung from the fields around Norfolk. Webster sampled these, and he tasted cherries for the first time. He would remember the tart juiciness of this delicious fruit, and how it made his mouth water.

The region's vegetables and fruits may have been nourished by the fertile soil, but its young minds were starving for knowledge. Towns throughout the South lagged far behind those in the North in educating the young. Families with means hired tutors and governesses to teach their offspring, but most children were illiterate. There were no common schools and it was against the law to teach enslaved people to read. "A shame to Virginia!" Webster cried. He left three dozen copies of his speller with a book vendor and hoped they would find buyers.

Sailing from Norfolk to Charleston, the *George* ran into squalls. Pitching, rolling, and buffeted by winds, the small craft fought to cover eight to twelve miles a day. A trip that should have taken a few days dragged on for three weeks. "O how disagreeable!" Webster complained. During the brief spells when the sea was calm, he joined the other passengers on deck for singing and dancing.

The *George* reached Charleston on Sunday, June 26, at eight in the morning, and Webster hurried off to church. He observed the polite citizens seated around him and nodded approvingly. "They behave with great decency in church," he remarked. It pleased him as well to see that the enslaved servants who came with their masters were also "remarkably attentive." These relatively well-treated household workers were a minority, however. Most of the South's enslaved African Americans toiled in the fields without rest. They lived in bare, tiny cabins and savored few if any of life's comforts.

Flames and cannon fire had destroyed much of Charleston during the Revolution. Some parts were still in ruins in 1785, but the people had rebuilt large sections of their city once peace returned. Waving mosquitoes away from his face, Webster strolled on brick sidewalks lining spacious streets and counted 1,540 houses. He saw tall church spires, and the three arched doorways of the Old Exchange Building, where the British housed prisoners during the war. "Charleston is very regular," he wrote in his diary.

A proud Webster showed the *Grammatical Institute* to leading city residents. He donated two hundred of his spellers and a hundred grammar books to the Mount Sion Society, a group that had opened a college nearby. The society's secretary praised this "production of a native of America at so early a period after her arduous and successful struggle for freedom."

Webster was still in Charleston on July 4, when the city celebrated American independence with fireworks and cannons. Some revelers launched an unmanned hot-air balloon that caught fire and fell onto the city market, but no one was hurt.

Webster recorded the numbers of houses he counted in the various cities that he visited.

Before the day was over, Webster climbed up into the steeple of St. Michael's Church. He looked down at the harbor, the city streets, and the farmland beyond. At that height, sea breezes blew across his face and through his hair, giving him some relief from the steamy South Carolina summer.

Traveling cost money, and Webster's was running out. He returned to Baltimore and searched for a way to support himself. He opened a language school, but no one came. He gave singing lessons and managed to attract ten students, but some were as strapped for cash as he was and

This picture shows Charleston between 1780 and 1782, when the city was under British control. Many of the buildings lining the waterfront would be damaged or destroyed as the British and Americans fought for control of the city.

paid him in gloves or shoes. Besides, the students had their own ideas about how to sing and sometimes argued with their instructor. "People in Baltimore have not been accustomed to my rigid discipline," he decided. He spent his twenty-seventh birthday feeling old and thinking gloomy thoughts. A year before, he had felt proud of his achievements. Now it seemed that life was speeding toward its end and he had yet to make his mark on the world. He wrote in his diary that the mere passing of a few years "sweeps us away!"

There had to be better ways to earn money, Webster thought. Maybe he could give lectures, like the Scottish scientist Henry Moyes. Moyes was on a speaking tour of the United States. In each city where he stopped, crowds paid to hear him lecture on chemistry and other scientific subjects. In Baltimore, Webster heard him speak about optics, the science of

light and lenses. Moyes had been born with great curiosity. Blinded by smallpox when he was only three, he had explored the world with his ears, nose, and fingers. His hands bore the scars of childhood experiments with tools.

After studying science at the University of Edinburgh, Moyes went on to become a leader in his field. Webster had been learning since boyhood too. Certainly he could lecture on language and education, he thought.

Eager to be the "American Dr. Moyes," Webster prepared five lectures and charged listeners a few shillings to hear them. On the evening of the first lecture, in October 1785, he stood in Baltimore's First Presbyterian Church watching a sparse audience straggle in from the rain. At seven o'clock, when he started to speak, just thirty pairs of eyes returned his gaze. He lectured that night on the wonders of English: "The English language," he professed, "is said to contain about 20,000 words. For the most part, the same idea, or nearly the same, may be expressed by two different words."

In later lectures Webster spoke about nouns, verbs, and the other parts of speech. He discussed such riveting subjects as long and short vowels. He lectured on the varied ways people in different parts of the

Between 1784 and 1786, the Scottish chemist Henry Moyes toured the United States, giving lectures.

country pronounced certain words. "Some of the southern people, particularly in Virginia, almost omit the sound of *r* as in *ware, there,*" he pointed out. He knew of no good reason for this omission. "It seems to be a habit contracted by carelessness," he said. Also, many people in the middle states were guilty of a "gross impropriety," he noted, because they "pronounce a *t* at the end of *once* and *twice,*" saying, "*oncet* and *twicet.*"

People are apt to make fun of others' odd ways of pronouncing words, Webster observed. This was a problem for the United States, because "a habit of laughing at the singularities of strangers is followed by disrespect," and friendship requires respect. Because Americans from different regions needed to work together as friends, "our political harmony is therefore concerned with a uniformity of language," he concluded.

No one knows exactly how spoken English sounded in Webster's time, but his lectures provide clues. For example, d-e-a-f was "generally pronounced *deef,*" he said, "tho some have adopted the English pronunci-ation, *def.*" He stated that *deaf* rhymed with *leaf* and *sheaf,* and had done so "from time immemorial." Perhaps this was so, but in the twenty-first century few Americans, if any, say "deef."

Webster gave his lectures in Maryland and Virginia. When he left the South in early 1786, he lectured as he ventured north, stopping in Dela-ware, Pennsylvania, New Jersey, and New York. In each place people liked his message, but they complained about the awkward way he delivered it. Webster "appears to be enraptured when he speaks, but his raptures seem forced. The motions of his hands are rather unpleasing," wrote one critic. Another dismissed him as a "know-it-all." A third complained that Webster's speaking style lacked "what are commonly called the flowers of rhetoric," the fancy figures of speech that many people looked forward to hearing from lecturers. "I wish to express my sentiments with clearness," Webster stated in his own defense.

On February 14, 1786, he reached Philadelphia, the nation's largest city. He counted 4,600 houses, from the small dwellings on Pine Street, crammed together without yards, to the towering mansions of Penn Street. He wandered down to the Delaware River, with its wharves broad enough to hold the cargoes of oceangoing ships.

Philadelphia was home to a number of famous Americans. Webster sought out Timothy Pickering, a former adjutant general of the Conti-nental Army. Pickering had sent him a letter praising the *Grammatical Institute* after purchasing it for his oldest son, John. "I am determined to have him instructed upon this new, ingenious, and at the same time easy

Thomas Paine was born in England, where he made ropes for ships and had a tobacco shop. He immigrated to North America in 1774 and soon gained fame for his political writing.

plan," Pickering had told his wife. The author, he said, "writes from his own experience as a schoolmaster, as well as the best authorities."

The influential Pickering introduced his new friend to Thomas Paine, the famed author of *Common Sense,* who was trying his luck as an inventor. Paine had come up with a candle that emitted its smoke through a hole at the bottom. He showed Webster a model of another project, an arched iron bridge that he had designed. He boasted that the bridge could span a river as wide as four hundred feet—which would have been a great feat of engineering in 1786. Paine would never prove his claim, because he could never convince anyone to build the bridge, just as he would never get anyone to make his candles.

Through Pickering, Noah also met the remarkable Benjamin Franklin—inventor, scientist, and patriot. Franklin had helped write the Declaration of Independence and had signed his name to it. He had persuaded France to enter the Revolution as America's ally. At eighty, Franklin was a short, heavyset, white-haired man who dressed plainly. He was still curious and eager to learn, and he had ideas for reforming the alphabet and spelling. If spelling was completely phonetic—if a word's spelling exactly matched its pronunciation—everyone could learn to spell, he insisted. And foreigners would know how to pronounce any

English word they saw printed in a book. Franklin thought he was too old to reform spelling on his own, so he asked Webster to help him.

While having dinner with the Pickerings one night, Webster met another signer of the Declaration of Independence. Benjamin Rush was a prominent physician who had published texts on scientific and medical subjects, from the cause and treatment of croup in children to the benefits of cold baths. Like Webster, Rush favored a national system of education to unify American culture. "Education alone will render the American Revolution a blessing to mankind," he wrote. Webster and Rush would become friends, although at first Rush thought the Connecticut

The physician Benjamin Rush, a signer of the Declaration of Independence and surgeon general of the Continental Army during the American Revolution, favored a national system of education to unify American culture.

schoolmaster seemed haughty. When he congratulated Webster on safely arriving in Philadelphia, he was startled by what Webster reportedly said: "Sir, you may congratulate Philadelphia on the occasion."

Did the women of Philadelphia find Noah Webster arrogant? "The Ladies will not dance with strangers, if they can avoid it—polite indeed!" Webster scoffed. Even if he failed to find romance at the Philadelphia balls, he at least gained the health benefits of dancing. "Its excellence consists in exciting a cheerfulness of the mind . . . in bracing the muscles of the body, and," he said, "in producing copious perspiration."

# CHAPTER 6

# A FRIEND TO HIS COUNTRY

IN 1786, from spring into fall, Webster lectured about language throughout New England. He spent a month in the West Division with his family and saw Joel Barlow, Nathan Perkins, and John Trumbull. On Thanksgiving he set out once more for Philadelphia, "to seek a living, perhaps for life," he said. His aging parents sadly watched him go, fearing they might not live to see him again. After stops in New Haven and New York, Noah completed his journey on Christmas Day. He rented a room in Mrs. Ford's boardinghouse and looked for a way to make money.

In January he announced that he would give seven lectures on language, government, and education. The lectures were "not designed for *amusement,*" he warned. Rather, they were for people with the "leisure and inclination to devote an hour to *serious* study." Is it any wonder that Philadelphians stayed away? While theaters offering musical entertainment filled their seats, Webster's hall sat sadly empty. He gave two lectures;

then, muttering about "the depraved taste" of Philadelphia's audiences, he canceled the rest of the series. Luckily for Noah, Timothy Pickering found him a job teaching English at the Episcopal Academy, a school for boys.

The people of Philadelphia knew of Noah Webster even if they had never heard him lecture. Word had gotten around that he thought pretty highly of himself, and he was joked about in the press. Webster's "consciousness of his own great learning and genius" had led him to think that he would become "one of the most valuable citizens of our new empire, and have his name ranked among the great men of this western world," gibed a newspaper writer who hid behind the pen name Seth. But, Seth noted, instead of achieving greatness, this person of "extraordinary knowledge and abilities" had taken the lowliest of jobs, "*to wit,* that of a schoolmaster."

The paper's next issue carried Webster's reply. His motives for teaching were "the noblest that can actuate the human mind," he stated. "This may be strange to *Seth,*" he continued, but then, "it is the character of blockheads to be gazing, and staring, and gaping at what they suppose *wonderful things;* but which appear to other people very common objects. It is probable, that *Seth* would be astonished to hear that ancient kings and sages taught children and schools—yet it is true."

Soon the post brought a letter from Noah's father. "I have had a hint son from some Gentlemen and some Newspapers as though you had made some Unfriendly to you by some of your writings and done your self damage," he wrote. "I would Caution you to be wise as a Serpent as well as harmless as a dove." It was good advice for someone who was hardly following in the path of ancient kings. Teaching school was a step backward for a man of twenty-eight who intended to make his mark on the world, and Noah Webster knew it. Still, he liked challenging young minds. Being a teacher came as naturally to him as thinking about language did.

As the nights grew cold, he started working with Benjamin Franklin on spelling reform. Soon, though, he faced a dilemma. Franklin was known for having smart ideas. He had given the world an efficient wood-burning stove and bifocal eyeglasses, which helped wearers see objects both far and near. He had devised experiments to expand people's knowledge of electricity. But Franklin's ideas about spelling were far from his best. He wanted to do away completely with the letters *c*, *j*, *w*, *x*, and *y*, which he called unnecessary. He claimed that their sounds could be represented by other letters, including some new ones he had invented. He gave these letters names like "ish" and "ing."

What had Noah gotten himself into? "Any scheme for introduction of a new alphabet, or new characters, is and will be impracticable," he believed. No one would use this new system, yet there was no easy way to back out of the project without hurting the old man's feelings. Besides, Webster liked Franklin and looked forward to spending more evenings with him. So he lied and said that if someday he had enough money to write and publish a dictionary, he would incorporate Franklin's notions on spelling.

BENJAMIN FRANKLIN

Né à Boston, dans la nouvelle Angleterre, le 17 Janv. 1706.

Benjamin Franklin shared Webster's enthusiasm for
spelling reform, but Webster thought some of Franklin's
ideas were too extreme.

Throughout the winter, Noah went to dinner parties and dances,
always noticing the young ladies and hoping for a glance his way. On
March 1, 1787, at the home of the Reverend James Sproat, pastor of
Philadelphia's Second Presbyterian Church, he met twenty-year-old
Rebecca Greenleaf of Boston. Rebecca was in town visiting a married
sister—O she was lovely! She was petite and slender, with hair as dark

as her nearly black eyes. And what was even more wondrous, she liked him! How glorious! Soon Rebecca was being escorted to concerts and gatherings by the strapping redheaded teacher and writer. They made a handsome couple, their Philadelphia friends agreed.

In June, when Rebecca went home to Boston carrying a lock of his hair, Noah felt heartbroken. He wrote to his "dear Becca," his "sweet girl," assuring her of his devotion to her happiness. The precious minutes spent writing to her, he confided, "revive your image in my mind and call into view your smiles, your friendship, and virtues." He wrote, *Without you* the world is all alike to me." He trusted each letter to the riders and wagon drivers who carried mail over the long, mostly unpaved roads that ran between Philadelphia and Boston, and he waited impatiently for her answers to come to him.

George Washington presides over the Constitutional Convention in this nineteenth-century woodcut.

It was difficult to be in love with Rebecca and so far away from her. Fortunately for Noah, something was happening in Philadelphia to distract him from his loneliness, something momentous. Delegates from twelve states had come together to write a new constitution for the United States, a strong one to replace the tottering

Articles of Confederation. Only Rhode Island declined to send representatives. Rhode Islanders feared that a more powerful national government might interfere with their state's profitable shipping trade.

The delegates spent sixteen weeks in the Pennsylvania State House, from May to September, debating and compromising. With hard work they hammered together the framework of a strong federal government with three branches: executive, legislative, and judicial. The leader of the executive branch, and of the nation, would be an elected president. The makeup of the legislative branch was a big subject for debate. Some states had more people than others, so the delegates had to find a way for each state — as well as each American — to be represented equally. They did this by dividing the legislative branch into two bodies, the House of Representatives and the Senate. The number of representatives a state elected to the House depended on its population. This gave each person an equal say. But each state had only two senators, giving them all the same voice in that body. The Supreme Court of the United States was the pinnacle of the judicial branch. Its justices had the power to decide whether laws passed by Congress and signed by the president were in keeping with the Constitution.

The controversial subject of slavery ignited heated arguments on the State House floor. Southern delegates, whose states' economies depended on the labor of enslaved African Americans, wanted slavery to continue under the new constitution. Enslaved workers raised tobacco and grain in Maryland and Virginia, and rice in South Carolina and Georgia. They made tar and turpentine in the pine forests of North Carolina.

Northerners viewed the issue differently. During the Revolution, most northern states had taken steps to end slavery within their borders. Connecticut, for example, passed a law in 1784 to abolish slavery gradually. Some northern delegates were willing to let slavery continue in states where it was legal if this would help forge a constitution everyone could accept. But others agreed with Gouverneur Morris, a Pennsylvania delegate, who condemned slavery as "the curse of heaven on the States where it prevailed."

After much debate, the Constitution would be silent on the legality of owning human beings. This meant that slavery would persist in the South. The Constitution did allow the enslaved population to be counted when determining how many representatives a state would have in Congress, though. Five enslaved people equaled three free Americans for the purpose of representation. This strange clause became known as the "three-fifths compromise."

The convention brought fifty-five outstanding men to Philadelphia. Webster had already met some of them, such as George Washington, who was presiding over the Constitutional Convention, and James Madison. That summer he shook hands with other delegates at dinner parties. He traded opinions with them on the future of the United States and its government, although the delegates kept their convention proceedings secret.

On August 22, he joined the delegates at the Schuylkill River. They had adjourned early that day to watch a coarse-mannered man named John Fitch demonstrate his new invention, a steam-powered boat. Fitch's craft, the *Perseverance,* moved upstream against the current at the astounding speed of three miles per hour. Fitch hoped to get financial backing to bring steamboat travel to America's rivers, but he never would find investors willing to take a chance on him. Instead

Webster stood in the crowd that marveled to see John Fitch's craft propelled over the water by its steam-powered oars.

of Fitch, the American engineer Robert Fulton is remembered for developing the first commercially successful steamboat, in 1807.

When he was not spending time with the delegates or writing letters to Rebecca, Webster worked on a new edition of his speller. The first thing he did was change its title to *The American Spelling Book.* It was time to drop Ezra Stiles's clunky title, which he had never liked. He arranged for a Philadelphia publisher to provide his schoolbooks to buyers in Pennsylvania, Virginia, Maryland, and Delaware, and to pay him a small royalty.

Soon summer ended, and on September 17, a clear, chilly day, the delegates voted to accept the new Constitution. Webster rejoiced, although he had hoped to see slavery abolished and a national system of education put in place. (Instead each state was to enact its own education laws.) Webster felt proud of his country—and of himself, because his *Sketches of American Policy,* with its call for power vested in the people, had shaped the delegates' thinking. He was sure of it. "I know of no other person who took the same active part or who devoted half the time to the subject which I did," he bragged.

Still, he wanted to do more. He was thrilled when Thomas Fitzsimmons, a delegate from Pennsylvania, asked for his help. At least nine states had to ratify, or vote to accept, the Constitution before it could become the law of the land. Fitzsimmons worried that opponents of the Constitution would convince their states to reject it. He asked Webster, "as a friend to your country," to persuade voters to support ratification.

It was the perfect task for someone who liked putting his opinions on paper. Webster sharpened a quill, dipped it in ink, and drafted a long letter to the citizens of the United States. A patient teacher, he explained what the Constitution meant and how the new government would work. He reassured readers that the system would benefit and protect them. "I firmly believe, that the life, liberty and property of every man, and the peace and independence of each state, will be more fully secured under such a constitution of federal government," he wrote. "Congress will have no more power than will be necessary for our union and general welfare; and such power they must have, or we are in a wretched state."

Webster admitted that readers were bound to find things they disliked in the Constitution, just as he did. "Perfection is not the lot of humanity," he noted. Yet when viewed as a whole, the system of freely elected leaders outlined in the Constitution was "the perfection of human government."

"A principal bulwark of freedom is the *right of election,*" Webster wrote. "Americans! Never resign that right." He signed his piece "A Citizen of America," and dedicated it to Benjamin Franklin. Titled *An Examination into the Leading Principles of the Federal Constitution,* it was distributed throughout the United States.

On October 27, 1787, ten days after Webster's pamphlet came off the press, a New York City newspaper printed the first of seventy-seven famous essays on the Constitution that would appear over the next year and a half. Authored by Alexander Hamilton, James Madison, and John Jay—a future secretary of the treasury, president of the United States, and chief justice of the Supreme Court—these essays are credited with persuading the nation to ratify the Constitution. Known as the Federalist Papers, they were written principally for men engaged in the world of commerce. Webster's pamphlet, composed in plain language that was easy to read, carried its message to ordinary people living on farms and in small towns. It was less well known, but it also had a wide influence.

It earned him no profit, however, and he desperately needed more money, because he wanted to marry Rebecca. Rebecca's father was a prosperous merchant who provided well for his wife and fifteen daughters and sons. Her future husband needed a steady, ample income if her parents were to approve of the match. The Episcopal Academy was paying Noah two hundred pounds a year in paper money, which was worth far less than its face value. He was earning some more from the sale of his schoolbooks, but not much. He faced the truth: he was poor, even if he kept his suits clean and well mended. He would have to find something better.

Benjamin Franklin had an idea, as he often did. His young friend should start a magazine, Franklin said. American readers loved magazines. In fact, people were launching new ones all the time. The most popular magazine, the *Columbian,* was produced right there in Philadelphia. Noah listened, because this idea of Franklin's sounded like a good one. Noah had something to say about nearly every subject. A magazine would be the perfect place to voice his opinions. What was more important, though, was this: his magazine could be useful for uniting the American people. He would design it "to gratify every class of readers," from clergymen and scholars to statesmen, merchants, and laborers. Why, it could even appeal to women! Noah was excited, but like everything he did, this magazine was to be a serious undertaking. "Ribaldry and immoral writings will form no part of the proposed selection," he cautioned.

Eager to get started, he resigned from his job at the Episcopal Academy, packed his trunk, and moved to New York City. With 3,340 houses, New York was smaller than Philadelphia, but it was a busier port. The many boats that embarked from New York every day could carry his magazine to towns up and down the Atlantic coast.

In January 1788, the first issue of Webster's *American Magazine* appeared. Then and in the months ahead, he filled its pages with news from home and abroad. He published poems by Joel Barlow, John Trumbull, and others. He borrowed stories from British publications, in-

New York City's Broadway was a busy thoroughfare in early America, just as it is today. This picture is from 1831.

cluding a tale by his hero, Samuel Johnson. He also composed many of the pieces himself. He often wrote about education, one of his favorite subjects. He wrote in support of public schooling for all American children: "The only practicable method to reform mankind is to begin with children," he claimed. "Education should therefore be the first care of a legislature—not merely the institution of schools, but furnishing them with the best men for teachers."

He signed some of his writing with made-up names, such as Peter Pickpenny and Guy Grumbleton. And despite his intention to be serious, some of these pieces were funny. For example, he wrote a letter to the editor from a distraught reader called Curiosus, who was asking for advice. Recently, at a ball, the sight of a beautiful woman had made Curiosus blush and stumble on the dance floor. He asked "whether a man is not excuseable for such mistakes." Webster, as editor, advised Curiosus "to become acquainted with the *Charming Girl,*" for "whether the attractions of beauty will excuse a man's unpoliteness, can be determined only by the charmers themselves."

In the May issue Webster published his "General Description of New York City," a portrait of the growing urban center as it was in 1788. Webster described streets broad and narrow, with and without sidewalks. "The most convenient and agreeable" of these, he observed, was Broadway. "This street is wide, and elevated so as to command a delightful prospect of the town, and the Hudson." He wrote about churches, government buildings, and the many brick houses with tiled roofs.

"New-York is one of the most social places on the continent," he noted. "The men collect themselves into weekly clubs. The ladies in winter are frequently entertained either at concerts of music, or assemblies, and make a very good appearance." If life in New York presented one "great inconvenience," it was "a want of good water," there being few wells in the city. "Most of the people are supplied every day with fresh water, conveyed to their doors in casks, from a pump near the head of Queen-street, which receives it from a pond, almost a mile from the city," Webster explained.

Noah sent copies of his magazine to his father, who wrote to him to say, "I think they are well written and will increase in credit as they are more known and read in the future." Noah Webster, Sr., then revealed that he had money worries by asking his son for a ten-pound loan.

# CHAPTER 7

# COXCOMB GENERAL OF THE UNITED STATES

ON JULY 23, 1788, New York City awakened to a joyful boom of cannons. Nine states had ratified the Constitution, transforming the document forged in Philadelphia into the law of the land. The city had prepared a great celebration—a grand procession—and it was time for people to take their places.

At ten o'clock, the parade began. With trumpets blaring, men on horseback led a mile and a half of marchers. Artillerymen, tradespeople, lawyers, physicians, the faculty and students of New York's Columbia College—they numbered five thousand in all. Another twenty thousand people lined the parade route. Boys waved and cheered. Girls and ladies leaned out windows or stood in open doorways.

"The march was slow and majestic," wrote Noah Webster, who treaded in its midst. He saw the city's skilled artisans carrying banners identifying themselves as horse doctors or confectioners, brush makers

New Yorkers turned out en masse to watch the parade celebrating ratification of the United States Constitution.

or butchers, stone masons or mathematical-instrument makers. Some craftsmen marched alongside horse-drawn floats. Webster noted that the float created by the cordwainers (shoemakers) portrayed "his excellency General Washington coming out of the State House at Philadelphia, and presenting the constitution to Fame, she receiving it standing in her temple, and ready to proclaim it to an astonished world!"

Webster rejoiced to see the states soundly united at last. Only one thing could make him happier, and in August it happened. He went to Boston and saw Rebecca again, after being apart from her for more than a year. She was as beautiful and devoted to him as ever, and the thought of another long separation was too much to bear. So he gathered up his nerve and asked Rebecca's father for her hand in marriage.

The Greenleafs liked Rebecca's suitor. They knew that the two young people cared deeply for each other and wanted to see them marry. Mr. Greenleaf could grant his permission only on one condition, though, and it was hardly a surprising one: Noah needed money. He would have to stop this silly business of writing and get serious about his career. Rebecca's father advised Noah to return to the practice of law, and to buckle down this time and make a success of it.

"The Federal plan most solid and sure / . . . Americans their freedom will ensure," proclaimed the orange silk flag carried by the pewterers, who forged pewter tankards as they paraded in New York City on July 23, 1788.

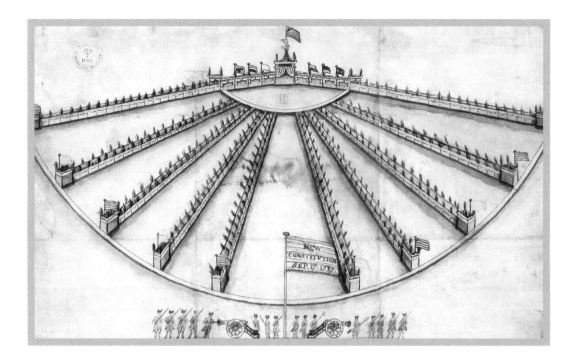

The procession in New York City led to a great banquet, where diners took their places at long tables arrayed like the spokes of a wheel. Dignitaries sat in the center. Webster reported that those present drank a series of toasts: to the Constitution; to George Washington; to the nation's European allies; to the soldiers who died defending liberty; to agriculture, manufacturing, science, trade, and navigation; and simply to the day. After each toast, ten cannons fired.

Noah felt a cloud form over his happiness. He had loved books and words since boyhood and had dreamed of making them his life's work. But if he and Becca were to have a future, then her father was right. He faced the fact that his *American Magazine* had never caught on with the public. Readers had quickly wearied of Webster's voice and Webster's opinions and wanted other points of view. When his birthday came he was in New York, getting the final issue ready for press and feeling low: "30 years of my life gone—a large portion of the ordinary age of man! I have read much, written much, & tried to do much good, but with little advantage," he wrote in his diary. "I am a bachelor & want the happiness of a friend whose interest & feelings should be mine." Once his business in New York was finished, he returned to Boston to try his luck as a lawyer—after he published one last book.

In *Dissertations on the English Language,* Webster collected the lectures he had given in American cities. At the book's end, he added an essay on spelling reform. In it he ignored Benjamin Franklin's made-up letters; instead he proposed ideas of his own to simplify spelling for Americans. He eliminated silent or extra letters from some words, turning *friend* into *frend,* for example, and *give* into *giv.* If certain letters made it hard to know how to pronounce a word, he replaced them with different letters that made the pronunciation clearer. He changed *daughter* into *dawter, grief* into *greef, blood* into *blud,* and *chorus* into *korus.*

These new spellings would benefit Americans of all ages, Webster believed. "It is now the work of years for children to learn to spell," he wrote. "Most people remain, all their lives, imperfect masters of spelling, and liable to make mistakes, whenever they take up a pen to write a short note." Under his new rules, it would be as difficult to spell incorrectly as it was to spell correctly with the old rules. Simpler spelling would also aid pronunciation. "All persons, of every rank, would speak with some degree of precision and uniformity," Webster explained. "Such a uniformity in these states is very desirable; it would remove prejudice, and conciliate mutual affection and respect."

Webster dedicated *Dissertations on the English Language* to Franklin, "a great Philosopher and a warm Patriot." He sent a copy of the

This miniature portrait of Noah Webster was painted in 1788, the year he turned thirty.

book to the old statesman in Philadelphia, who replied with a letter of thanks. Franklin, who would die the next year, called Webster's *Dissertations* "an excellent work," one that "will be greatly useful in turning the thoughts of our countrymen to correct writing."

The proposed spelling changes would reduce the number of letters a writer used by one-eighteenth, Webster calculated. They would therefore lessen the number of pages in a book by the same fraction. "A saving of an eighteenth in the expense of books, is an advantage that should not be overlooked," he pointed out. No one knew this better than Webster himself, who had paid for *Dissertations on the English Language* to be printed. The book sold poorly, and he was out four hundred dollars just when he could least afford to lose money.

If only he would prosper as a lawyer — but his search for legal work in Boston turned up nothing. He had better try again in Hartford, where people knew him, Rebecca's parents said. Noah hated to leave Boston, where he sat by Rebecca's side at dinners and teas. Through the Greenleafs he had met some of Boston's elite, including John Adams, who was soon to be the first vice president. But he was in no position to go against the wishes of his future in-laws, so in May 1789 he parted from Rebecca for what they hoped would be a short while.

Back in Hartford, he rented a room in John Trumbull's house for ten pence a week. He was glad to see Pastor Nathan Perkins and other old friends, but he still had trouble finding enough work to get ahead. Hartford had no shortage of lawyers, just as before, and most people employed the attorneys who had served their families for years. Noah told himself that in a few years his practice would improve. Unhappy and bored, he made humdrum entries in his diary, noting that he went to church, that he started bathing in the morning instead of at night, that he went to see his family.

Then, in August, a letter arrived, bringing him unexpected joy. Rebecca's brother James, who lived in the Netherlands with his Dutch wife, was sending Noah a thousand dollars to hurry along the wedding. James Greenleaf had made his own fortune buying and selling land. His gift was an extremely generous one, roughly equal to $27,000 in the second decade of the twenty-first century. It was enough to get newlyweds started in life—if they lived frugally. Writing to James in thanks, Noah praised his future wife. "If there ever was a woman, moulded by the hand of nature to bless her friends in all connections, it is your sister," he gushed. The man lucky enough to share his life with Rebecca "must become a better man, a better citizen, a warmer friend." He rented a house in the center of Hartford, and on October 17 he rushed back to Boston to marry his bride.

As soon as he arrived, he came down with the flu. The wedding would have to wait. He dared not step out even to see George Washington, who had been sworn in as president six months before. The nation's new leader was touring Connecticut and Massachusetts and was honoring Boston with a visit. Wearing his general's uniform, Washington watched from the balcony of the Massachusetts State House on October 24, 1789, as the city's artisans and schoolchildren paraded in his honor. That night fireworks exploded in the sky over Boston, and every public house in the city glowed with celebratory light.

By Monday morning, October 26, Noah felt better. "This day I became a husband," he noted in his diary. Summing up his life, he wrote,

The people of Boston built this triumphal arch and colonnade for
George Washington to pass under when parading through their city.

"I begin a profession, at a late period of life, but have some advantages
of traveling and observation. I am united to an amiable woman, & if I
am not happy, shall be much disappointed." James Greenleaf sent good
wishes from the Netherlands: "That you may live *long & enjoy* every *day*,
every *hour* of your lives is my hearty prayer."

When Noah and Rebecca Webster left for Hartford to begin their
married life, Rebecca's sister Priscilla came along to stay awhile and help
them settle into their new home. On November 26, Thanksgiving, the
sisters cooked up a great feast. They prepared "eleven pumpkins puddings, three plump pudding, & seven apple pyes," reckoned Rebecca, an

imperfect master of spelling. "Webster & Priss have demolished all the pumkin puddings & begin to make a hugh & cry after more," she wrote to her brother John, in Boston.

Rebecca told John that Noah had taken her to meet his family. "Mr. Webster's mother shed tears when she saw me for the first time," she wrote. "Most of the family were together; the little children crouded round their new aunt & admird her cloaths (for you must know I had on my green brocade)." The meeting was strained. Mercy Webster was shocked to learn that her new daughter-in-law had never learned to knit. Rebecca was repelled by one of the family's customs, possibly their habit of spitting on the floor. Whatever it was, Noah made sure his family stopped it at once.

As a Boston lady in green brocade—a rich man's daughter—Rebecca had yet to learn to live on a budget. She bought costly chintz-covered furniture, fine china, and mirrors to hang on the walls, and pretty soon the thousand dollars from James Greenleaf had been spent. Noah had to ask his brother-in-law for more money, in the form of a loan. When spring came, he economized by planting a kitchen garden. A farmer's son, he raised beets, carrots, cucumbers, parsnips, and potatoes. Years later, when he wrote his dictionary, Webster defined the humble "potatoe" as "one of the greatest blessings bestowed on man by the Creator."

Little by little, lawyerly work came his way. He drafted legal documents for clients, and he was employed by Jedediah Strong, the judge with whom he had lived while studying law. Since he and Webster last parted, Strong had been the subject of sensational newspaper reports, having been arrested for cruel treatment of his second wife, Susannah. The couple had divorced, and Strong wanted Susannah to release her claim to her dower—the share of his estate she was to receive upon his death. Webster did all he could as an attorney, but Susannah rejected the request. It later became clear that Strong was slipping into insanity, and in 1798 a court appointed a guardian to oversee his affairs. Webster remained his loyal friend until Strong's death in 1802.

Webster was doing something else besides lawyering—he was writing. Despite his promise to Rebecca's father, he simply had to write. He authored an anonymous pamphlet about Connecticut's new sales tax on imported goods, explaining why it was unconstitutional. His argument swayed enough state legislators to get the tax repealed. He wrote a series of essays on the English language for a Hartford newspaper, and in June 1790 he published another book, *A Collection of Essays and Fugitiv Writings.*

In this volume Webster collected several "Peeces" he had "ritten at various times, and on different occasions." Most had "appeered before in periodical papers and Magazeens." In this gathering of earlier writings, he changed the spelling of many words, experimenting with his phonetic system. As a result, most readers paid less attention to what he wrote than to how the words looked. Some liked Webster's changes and thought they might help poor spellers, but others found them laughable. No one thought they were funnier than the Reverend Jeremy Belknap, founder of the Massachusetts Historical Society. He ridiculed this new system of spelling recommended by "*No-ur Webster eskwier junier,* critick and coxcomb general of the United States."

Webster failed to see the humor. It was "doubtful," he concluded, "whether the public mind is prepared for a reformed plan of spelling."

On May 31, 1790, right before Webster's book entered the world, President Washington signed the first national copyright law. It protected an author's work throughout the United States for fourteen years and permitted the author to renew the copyright for another fourteen. To Webster, this law was long overdue. His schoolbooks could be found throughout the country, but they were being printed by at least five publishers in cities from Philadelphia to Bennington, Vermont. He made a new deal with the Boston firm of Thomas and Andrews. As his contracts with all the other publishers expired, Thomas and Andrews would take over that share of the business. For the next twenty-eight years (two fourteen-year copyright terms), they would be the principal publisher of Webster's schoolbooks for the entire United States.

Thomas and Andrews also published Webster's next book, *The Prompter,* which turned out to be popular with readers. A prompter is the person who sits offstage during a play and whispers lines to actors who have forgotten them. "A Prompter then says but *little,* but that much little is *very necessary* and often does *much good,*" Webster wrote. "The writer of this little Book took it into his head to *prompt* the numerous actors upon the great theatre of life."

Webster displayed his wit and wisdom in these commentaries on popular sayings. About the often-said "I told you so," he observed, "What a wise man is this I . . . he struts and says with a boasting superiority, *I told you so,* though perhaps he never said a word about it until the thing happened." The adage "When a man is going down hill, every one gives him a kick" was true for two reasons, Webster remarked. "First, it is much easier to kick a man *down hill,* than to push him *up hill;* Second, men love to see every body at the bottom of the hill but *themselves.*" He issued a warning about young people "sowing *wild oats.*" It was all well and good for the young to have fun, he stated, but they had to beware lest their amusements turn into vices. "Habit sticks fast to a man, like his skin," he cautioned.

On August 4, 1790, Noah and Rebecca welcomed their first child, a daughter named Emily. Rebecca's mother and father had come from Boston for the occasion, so all four of Emily's grandparents were on hand to celebrate. Even as a tiny baby Emily loved the sound of her father's flute. Its music was the one sound that could always be relied on to quiet her crying.

Emily Webster was the child of a busy man. Noah was constantly tending to his legal work, his writing, and his civic duties. He served on Hartford's common council and helped found the Hartford Bank and the Connecticut Society for the Abolition of Slavery. He was active in the Charitable Society of Hartford, which aided the poor, although he and Rebecca were still short of money.

In fact, when financial hardship forced his parents to sell their farm and move in with Noah's sister Mercy and her husband, they could offer no help. Even their joy at the birth of their second daughter, Frances Juliana (called Julia) on February 5, 1793, was dampened by money worries. By then Noah and Rebecca were more than eighteen hundred dollars in debt.

All through the hot summer of 1793, Noah racked his brains, desperate to think of a way to make money. Some days he thought he might turn his back on all he had been trying to do—the writing, the law, the active citizenship—and become a simple farmer. Other days, he could see himself running a bookstore.

That fall, a solution came from the world of politics. Treasury Secretary Alexander Hamilton and other leading Federalists wanted to use the press to get their ideas across to the American public. They loaned Webster the money to start a newspaper.

# CHAPTER 8

# COMPILER OF FACTS

IN 1793, America was full of talk about a foreign war. France had declared war on England and Spain, and the question being debated was this: Should the United States support one side or the other? Many Americans felt a duty to the French, who had helped them win the War for Independence. Others, still loyal to Britain, saw this war as a chance to reunite the former colonies and their mother country. There were also those, including Washington, who were determined to stay neutral. The president knew that the United States had neither the funds nor the military might to take part in this war.

France was also experiencing a tumultuous revolution of its own. It had begun in 1789, with the poor, hungry populace storming Paris's Bastille prison, a symbol of royal authority, and murdering public officials. Noah Webster rejoiced in 1792, when a freely elected National

Convention established the First French Republic. Then the new government's powerful Committee of Safety launched the Reign of Terror. Determined to eliminate every enemy, they beheaded the king and queen and thousands of noblemen and -women. Webster still supported the French goals of liberty and equality, but he deplored the violence of the French Revolution. He told himself that the French were "creating some evils to correct enormous abuses" and hoped this was true.

The French ambassador to the United States, Edmond-Charles Genêt, was doing all he could to bring the United States into the war with Britain and Spain. In Charleston, "Citizen" Genêt outfitted warships and sent them to attack British and Spanish merchant vessels. He stirred up anger in Georgia against the Spanish forces in Florida, to the south. Genêt addressed eager crowds in New York City. Handsome, young, and persuasive, he had his audiences chanting, "*Vive* Ge-nêt!" (Long live Genêt!)

The Federalist newspaper that Webster was going to edit, the *American Minerva,* was being founded partly to combat Genêt. Webster met Genêt by chance when he was in New York on business related to his books, and was dining at an inn. Their polite conversation quickly turned into a shouting match, with Webster calling Genêt a madman and hurling swear words he had learned in college from Joel Barlow. "I cannot with propriety state all I said myself on that occasion," Webster told his friend Oliver Wolcott.

In October, Webster said goodbye forever to the practice of law and moved with his wife and daughters to New York City. Rebecca's brother

Ambassador Edmond-Charles Genêt pays a formal call on President George Washington in this magazine illustration from 1897. Protocol demanded that Genêt present himself to Washington soon after arriving in the United States, but Genêt delayed the obligation for several weeks as he stirred up American support for France.

James Greenleaf, who was back in the United States, found the family a house to rent on Queen Street (renamed Pearl Street in 1794). The house was roomy enough for James to have an office there as well. He had left his wife and children in the Netherlands and would soon divorce.

James was involved in a big venture, buying up lots in the new capital city, Washington, D.C. Houses and government buildings would one day sit on this land, which he expected to sell at a huge profit.

Settled in New York, Noah immediately got to work. By December 1793, he was publishing his four-page newspaper six days a week — every day but Sunday. In June 1794, he started a second, smaller paper that came out twice a week and was meant for readers outside New York. He mailed the *Herald: A Gazette for the Country* to bookstores in other states. He also shipped it to Europe, so readers there could have news from America. Unable to pay an assistant, Webster did nearly all the work himself, from proofreading the printed pages to keeping the accounts. He put aside his diary — no time! A neighbor saw him as a man with a purpose, "with keen gray eyes and sharply cut features," who "was remarkable for his erect walk and perfection of neatness in dress."

For the *American Minerva,* Webster covered the French Revolution by translating news from foreign papers and writing his own editorials. He wrote about slavery, sanitation, and other domestic issues. He promoted his schoolbooks and printed words of praise for his book *The Prompter,* claiming, "Many householders deem it so useful as to purchase a copy for every adult in their families."

And, of course, he wrote about Genêt. He warned, "Never will the brave freemen of our Republic permit the secret influence or open forces of a foreign nation to dictate to them what measures to pursue." Genêt's star was already fading in the United States and in France, though. Soon the ruthless French government, unhappy with his failure to gain U.S.

support, issued a warrant for his arrest and demanded his return. Genêt knew that being arrested in France almost certainly meant being sent to the guillotine. So he appealed to Washington for political asylum, and the president granted it. Genêt married an American woman and began a new life as a gentleman farmer on Long Island.

After moving to New York, Webster rarely wrote letters to his own family of farmers. He had grown apart from them and had little to say to them anymore. After his mother died of dysentery in October 1794, Noah heard from his father only when the older man wrote to ask for money.

This picture of Noah Webster, which appeared in an early edition of his spelling book, is known as the "porcupine portrait."

The friendly relationship that Noah and Rebecca had enjoyed with her brother James also came to an end. James Greenleaf had abused the Websters' kindness by inviting in friends for loud nights of drinking whenever he was in town, and leaving messes for others to clean up. "Becca is compelled to become a servant herself," Noah scolded his brother-in-law. "You cannot conceive how unhappy you make her." It came to light that James was making crooked deals and stealing money from his business partners. He would lose his wealth and spend a year in debtors' prison. "Thanks to my good fortune, I quarreled myself out of his clutches," Noah wrote to Rebecca's brother Daniel at that time.

In 1795 the *American Minerva* took up a new cause. Yellow fever had come to New York City. This frightening illness gave the eyes and skin a yellowish cast. It caused patients to bleed into their stomachs and vomit dried, black blood. As organs failed one after another—the liver, kidneys, and heart—many victims died. The first case appeared in July, and seven hundred thirty-two New Yorkers perished before the outbreak ended four months later. Wealthy residents fled the city to wait out the epidemic in the country.

No one knew what caused yellow fever, but many people blamed filth. They pointed to dirty cellars and yards, piles of rotting vegetables, and foul privies and sewers. Benjamin Rush, the Philadelphia doctor, claimed that being too hot or too cold, getting tired out from walking or swimming, or eating too much ice cream made a person more likely to catch yellow fever.

When yellow fever raged through Philadelphia two years earlier, Rush had prescribed bloodletting—removing up to a quart of a patient's blood each day from an open vein—and high doses of mercury, a toxic metal. It is not surprising that neither treatment helped anyone. Believing African Americans had a natural immunity to the disease,

The *American Minerva*, which Noah Webster began publishing on December 9, 1793, was New York City's first daily newspaper. Minerva was the Roman goddess of wisdom.

Philadelphia enlisted its free black population to treat the sick and carry away the dead. It became clear, however, that yellow fever spared neither blacks nor whites.

"As *facts* are the basis of human knowledge, it is of great importance to collect them," Webster believed. If enough experts pooled information, then the nation might better understand this mysterious disease. In his newspapers he called on physicians to share their observations. How did the fever begin in their cities? Was it contagious, as many people believed? Had any treatments worked? "The world is a book of instruction," Webster wrote. It made sense to profit from its lessons.

He printed letters from physicians as they arrived in the mail, but each doctor seemed to disagree with all the others. If Webster published a letter from a physician who claimed that cleanliness and a meatless diet cured yellow fever, another doctor would write to recommend camphor, enemas, and cold showers. A third would then fire off an angry letter to point out that camphor irritates the nostrils. The doctors' bickering was starting to sound crazy. "Is not a partial delirium discernible in their writings and challenges?" Webster asked.

Instead of printing any more letters in the *American Minerva,* he compiled the physicians' responses in a book, *A Collection of Papers on the Subject of Bilious Fevers.* Based on what the doctors wrote, he concluded that contamination, especially rotting vegetables and meat and the putrid air around them, caused yellow fever. "It is as much the *duty* of the citizens of populous towns, to cleanse their streets, and their back yards, wash their houses and bathe their persons, as it is to provide a Hospital for the indigent sick, or a grave for the dead," he wrote. (Nearly a century was to pass before a team led by the U.S. Army physician Walter Reed proved that mosquitoes transmit the bacteria that cause yellow fever.)

In spring 1796, alarmed at the kitchen slops and dead rodents fouling the air in city streets, Noah and Rebecca Webster moved their family a mile north to Corlear's Hook, a section of Manhattan Island that was still countrified. Their house overlooked the East River, and they had land enough for a garden and a horse, which Noah rode to his office each day. If a stray cat wandered up to the door, the Websters always took it in. A year after the move, a third daughter, Harriet, was born.

Noah was making enough money to employ an assistant in his office, but he had grown bored with newspaper work. "I am fatigued with narrating the absurdities of man," he admitted. He craved a bigger challenge. He had been thinking about lexicography — dictionary writing. He dreamed of bringing together in one book the correct spelling, pronunciation, and definition of every word Americans used. In the past he had been too poor to take on such an ambitious project; now, at last, the time seemed right. In spring 1798, he hired an editor to take over his duties at the newspaper, although he would contribute articles from time to time. "My plan of education is but barely *begun*," he declared.

The Websters moved to New Haven and bought a two-story white house that had once belonged to Benedict Arnold. Since leading Yale students in a raid at the start of the Revolution, Arnold had become

LE GENERAL ARNOLD un des Chefs de l Armée Anglo Americaine

Benedict Arnold was an American general and a hero of the Revolution when this French portrait was printed, in the 1770s. In 1780 his treasonous plan to surrender the fort at West Point, New York, came to light, and he fled to England.

notorious. As an officer in the Continental Army, he rose to the rank of major general. In August 1780, Washington placed him in command of the garrison at West Point, New York. But Arnold had secretly switched sides, and was spying for the enemy. When his plot to surrender West Point was exposed, he fought openly for the British. By 1798 he was living in London.

The "Benedict Arnold House" was to be the Websters' home for the next fifteen years. Noah planted cherry trees on the grounds, recalling the delicious taste of their fruit, as well as peach trees and flowers. Although his children went to school, he was often their teacher at home, instructing them in spelling, reading, arithmetic, and science. Ever a music lover, he taught them to sing and play the flute. He thought about their education even when he was far away. Writing to them while traveling in New York State, he described the course of his journey. "Such is my progress my dear girls and you must take your maps and trace it out," he directed. "It will help you to remember the geography of this country."

He still left home to promote his books, but these days Webster spent more and more time in his second-floor study, with the door closed against the voices of callers and the happy clamor of his girls at play. He passed satisfying hours with paper and pen, gathering facts and putting them in order. He looked forward to starting his dictionary, but first he wanted to learn more about disease.

Like yellow fever, other serious, sometimes fatal illnesses had arisen in the United States and Europe. Noah remembered the influenza that kept him in bed and delayed his wedding. He thought of scarlet fever, which snatched away many children in the eighteenth century. His own daughters had survived mild infections in 1794. Bubonic plague,

The Benedict Arnold House in New Haven, where the Websters lived from 1798 until 1812, was for sale when it was photographed in 1891. The house was torn down in 1917.

smallpox, typhus, diphtheria—there were so many diseases to learn about and so many facts discover. Noah searched libraries in New Haven, Philadelphia, and Cambridge, Massachusetts. He spent months reading everything he could find. He even tracked down an early account of smallpox and plague among New England's Indians. "Facts which were new to me were daily presenting themselves to my mind," he said. "I was persuaded that those facts are of too much importance to philosophy, to medicin and to human happiness, not to merit publication."

In 1798 he came down with yellow fever himself, after a brief trip to

New York City. He escaped the worst symptoms, but he was sick for ten weeks and felt weak for months afterward. He kept working during his illness and recovery, and in 1799 he published *A Brief History of Epidemic and Pestilential Diseases.* More than seven hundred pages long, this book was anything but brief. In it Webster traced the history of disease in the Western world, beginning in the year A.D. 40, when outbreaks of plague seemed to coincide with earthquakes and comets. About a recent appearance of yellow fever in Connecticut he wrote, "The spot where this fever arose, is low ground, retaining water to stagnate after the spring floods." Garbage and rotting vegetation collected at this spot, confirming for Webster the notion that the fever arose from filth.

The Websters' fourth daughter, Mary, was born on January 7, 1799. On December 14 of that year, as bright-eyed Mary was starting to toddle, George Washington died. The beloved president had retired to Mount Vernon at the close of his second term. "All America Mourns," Webster noted. He wrote to Washington's heir, his nephew Bushrod Washington, and asked for permission to be the first president's official biographer. But Bushrod Washington gave the job to John Marshall, a future chief justice of the Supreme Court.

It was just as well, because Webster needed to buckle down and start compiling his dictionary. First, though, he wanted to write something else: an encyclopedia for America's children. Youngsters should be learning more about the world and the sciences, he believed. For this reason he filled *Elements of Useful Knowledge* with information on the solar

Americans mourning the death of their first president could buy this memorial print. The figure to the left is Columbia, mourning the loss of her son. The other figure, Fame, is spreading the sad news of Washington's death.

system, history and geography, and the animal kingdom. The first volume was published in 1802.

Webster liked children and took pleasure in seeing them learn. He was overjoyed on September 15, 1801, when his first son was born. He and Rebecca christened the boy William. With four daughters and a son, the Websters had half the ten children Noah hoped for.

Around the time of William's birth, Noah received a letter from Eliphalet Steele, his mother's younger brother. "Have you completed your dictionary?" Noah's uncle wanted to know.

Completed his dictionary? He had barely begun!

# CHAPTER 9

# MIXING WEEDS AND FLOWERS

ON JUNE 4, 1800, Webster had announced in the *Connecticut Journal* his plan to write a dictionary. An American dictionary was needed, he explained, "on account of differences between the American and English language. New circumstances, new modes of life, new laws, new ideas of various kinds give rise to new words." He predicted, "The differences in the languages of the two countries will continue to multiply and render it necessary that we should have Dictionaries of the American Language." Webster understood that "a living language," one people use in daily life, was going to evolve. It "must keep pace with improvements in knowledge and with the multiplication of ideas," he wrote. Some words would be invented to fill a need, and others would take on new meanings.

To most people at the time, the thought of new words entering a dictionary sounded ridiculous. English was English, they insisted, in

America and overseas, and the English used by learned people needed to be preserved for future generations. If every new word found its way into a dictionary, then the language would be burdened with strange, obscure terms. A new dictionary might have to be issued every year!

Noah Webster was a "mortal and incurable lunatic," claimed one of his critics. Would Webster please "turn his mind from language-making to something really useful"? asked another. "If, as Mr. Webster asserts, it is true that many new words have already crept into the language of the United States," remarked someone else, "he would be much better employed in rooting out those anxious weeds, than in mingling them with the flowers."

Webster knew he was out of step with most people. "Either from the structure of my mind or from my modes of investigation, I am led very often to differ in opinion from many of my respectable fellow citizens," he said. He would do best, he knew, to "withdraw myself from every public concern and confine my attention to private affairs and the education of my children." So he shut his study door against the critics and focused on words, his loyal friends.

English authors had been producing word books and dictionaries since the 1400s. The first ones defined English words in Latin, which was then the language of scholars and scribes. In the 1600s dictionaries with English definitions appeared, but they contained only hard and unusual words, because everyone knew the meanings of easy, everyday ones. Over time, writers produced dictionaries that were longer and more complete. In 1755, Webster's favorite author, Samuel Johnson, had published one of the most famous, *A Dictionary of the English Language*. Johnson's work was huge for its day. He wrote definitions for more than forty-two thousand words, and he often did so in a new way, by including quotations from great writers to clarify meanings. For example, after defining the verb *to affront* as "to meet face to face; to encounter," he offered these lines from Shakespeare's *Hamlet*:

> *We have closely sent for Hamlet hither,*
> *That he, as 'twere by accident, may here*
> Affront *Ophelia.*

More recently, American dictionaries had begun to appear. A Connecticut schoolteacher published the first comprehensive one, *A School Dictionary,* in 1798. His name happened to be Samuel Johnson, Jr., but he was not related to the famed British author. In his small book intended for students, this Samuel Johnson gave brief definitions of 4,150 words. He seemed to follow the example of seventeenth-century lexicographers, because he included such uncommon words as *cognomen, dominical,* and *tweedle,* but left out ordinary terms such as *algebra, balloon,* and *ocean.*

He then teamed up with a Yale-educated minister, the Reverend John Elliott, to produce a larger, improved version in 1800. *A Selected Pronouncing and Accented Dictionary* contained seven thousand more definitions than the earlier book. It was the first dictionary to include Native American words such as *wampum* and *tomahawk,* as well as names of American places.

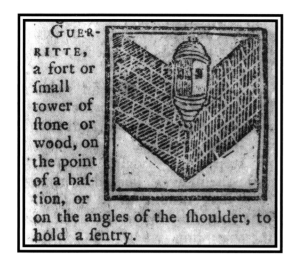

GUER- RITTE, a fort or ſmall tower of ſtone or wood, on the point of a baſtion, or on the angles of the ſhoulder, to hold a ſentry.

This definition is from *A New Military, Historical and Explanatory Dictionary*, by Thomas Simes, a guidebook for army officers printed in Philadelphia during the American Revolution. It was one of very few dictionaries produced in America before Webster's appeared.

Webster turned his attention to his own dictionary, but he never could write a book without distracting himself. He was in Philadelphia in December 1803, overseeing the printing of a new, revised spelling book, when his daughter Eliza was born in New Haven.

He also put aside the dictionary to publish newspaper articles aimed at President Thomas Jefferson, who was sworn in on March 4, 1801. Jefferson opposed the Federalist policies that Webster held dear, and his Democratic-Republican Party favored strong state governments. It was too friendly toward France, in Webster's opinion, and had opposed the 1794 Jay Treaty, which promoted trade and friendship between the United States and Britain. It was no wonder Webster felt disgruntled!

In his articles he lectured Jefferson directly and the more he wrote, the angrier he became. "In groping thro the dark labyrinth of your professions and conduct, we find scarcely a ray of reason," he railed. "Your administration will sink you to the rank which correct observers have long ago assigned you; that of a superficial philosopher, more showy than profound—an ambitious, but weak politician." He went on like this for

The artist who created this portrait of Thomas Jefferson portrayed the third president wearing a laurel wreath, an ancient symbol of a triumphant leader.

page after page, at one point lamenting, "To what a state of degradation has the government fallen!"

Jefferson was impressed, but not favorably. "I view Webster as a mere pedagogue, of very limited understanding and very strong prejudices and party passions," he coolly remarked to James Madison.

Webster was passionate, all right—about politics and about words. Writing his dictionary was a bigger job than he had ever imagined, one that grew bigger by the day. "The field of inquiry enlarges with every step I take," he told one of his many brothers-in-law. Finally, in 1806, he published *A Compendious Dictionary of the English Language*.

Something compendious packs a lot of information into a small package. Webster's dictionary was small, just six and a half inches from top to bottom, and four inches across. In it he had defined forty thousand words, including five thousand new ones. These included medical and scientific terms, such as *vaccination* and *chlorite;* words pertaining to the U.S. government and monetary system, such as *presidential* and *cent;* and adjectives formed from proper nouns—*Newtonian,* for example. Again he altered spelling, but the changes he proposed this time were more moderate than some he had tried before. He removed the *u* from words such as *honour* and *favour,* spelling them *honor* and *favor.* He changed

EMI    [—101—]    EMU

Em'baffage, Em'baffy, *n.* a public meffage or truft
Embat'tle, *v. t.* to fet or range in order of battle
Embáy, *v. t.* to inclofe in a bay, wafh, bathe
Embel'lifh, *v. t.* to adorn, trim, beautify, fet off
Embel'lifhment, *n.* ornament, decoration, grace
Em'bers, *n. pl.* hot cinders, afhes not yet dead
Embez'zle, *v. t.* to defraud by appropriating to *one's own ufe,* what is entrufted to one's care,
Embez'zlement, *n.* fraud by ufing anothers prop-
· erty for one's own benefit
Emblázon, *v. t.* to blazon, adorn, paint, defcribe
Em'blem, *n.* a moral device, reprefentation, token
Em'blem, *v. t.* to reprefent or defcribe allufively
Emblemat'ical, *a.* ufing emblems, allufive
Emblemat'ically, *ad.* allufively, with allufion
Emblem'atift, *n.* a writer or inventor of emblems
Em'blements, *n. pl.* the produce from fown land
Em'bolifm, *n.* an intercalation, a time inferted
Embofs', *v. t.* to adorn with rifing work, to inclofe
Embofs'ing, *n.* the art of making figures in relievo
Embofs'ment, *n.* relief, rifing work, a fculpture
Embot'tle, *v. t.* to include in bottles, to bottle up
Embow'el, *v. t.* to take out the entrails, to gut
Embráce, *v. t.* to fqueeze, take, comprife
Embráce, Embrácement, *n.* a clafp, hug, crufh
Embrácery, *n.* an attempt to influence a jury cor-
ruptly      (a jury
Embrácing, *n.* the crime of attempting to corrupt
Embrafúre, *n.* a battlement, an opening in a wall
Em'brocate, *v. t.* to foment or rub a part difeafed
Embrocátion, *n.* fomentation, rubbing, lotion
Embroid'er, *v. t.* to adorn with figure-work
Embroid'erer, *n.* a perfon who works embroidery
Embroid'ery, *n.* a fort of variegated needlework
Embroil', *v. t.* to difturb, confufe, involve, broil
Embroth'el, *v. t.* to fhut in a brothel, *ob.*
Embrúted, *a.* reduced to brutality, very depraved
Em'bryo, Em'bryon, *n.* the rudiments of an ani-
mal or plant, before the parts are diftinctly
formed, the beginning
Em'bryon, *a.* pertaining to firft rudiments
Emendátion, *n.* a correction, alteration, change
Em'erald, *n.* a gem, a kind of green precious ftone
Emerge', *v. i.* to iffue, to rife out of, from or up
Emer'gency, *n.* a rifing out of, preffing neceffity
Emer'gent, *a.* coming out or into fight, fudden
Em'erods, *n.* the piles
Emer'fion, *n.* the act of rifing out of water, a rife
Em'ertis, *n.* plain India muflins, thin and of infe-
rior quality, about 7 8ths in width
Em'ery, *n.* a kind of iron ore, a glazier's diamond
Emet'ic, *a.* that provokes vomiting ; *n.* a vomit
Emication, *n.* the act of fparkling or glittering
Emiction, *n.* urine, the making of urine    [away
Em'igrant, *a.* going from place to place, moving
Em'igrant, *n.* a perfon who quits his own country
to refide in another
Em'igrate, *v. i.* to remove from place to place
Emigrátion, *n.* a change of habitation or place·

Em'inence, *n.* height, honor, top, a cardinal's title
Em'inent, *a.* high, lofty, remarkable, celebrated
Em'inently, *ad.* confpicuoufly, in a high degree
E'mir, *n.* a Turkifh prince, Vizer or Bafhaw
Em'iffary, *n.* a fecret agent, agent, fpy, fcout
Emiſ'fion, *n.* a throwing out, a vent, a fhooting
Emit', *v.* to dart, let fly, fend out, iffue out, dif-
Em'met, *n.* a kind of infect, ant, pifmire   (charge
Emmew', *v. t.* to mew, fhut or coop up, *ob.*
Emmóve, *v. t.* to move, ftir or roufe up, *ob.*
Emolles'cence, *n.* foftnefs, or the loweft degree of
fufibility in bodies
Emol'lient, *a.* foftening, fuppling, moiftening
Emol'lient, *n.* a medicin which foftens
Emolli'tion, *n.* the act of foftening or relaxing
Emol'ument, *n.* profit, gain, advantage, benefit
Emolument'al, *a.* ufeful, producing emolument
Emótion, *n.* a fudden motion, difturbance of mind
Empále, *v. t.* to inclofe, fortify, fence in, put on a
ftake            (flower
Empálement, *n.* a fixing on a ftake, the calyx of a
Empéople, *v.* to form into a community, *ob.*
Em'peror, *n.* a monarch, a title fuperior to king
Em'phafis, *n.* a remarkable ftrefs laid on a word
Em'phafize, *v. t.* to pronounce with a ftrefs of voice
Emphat'ical, *a.* ftrong, forcible, ftriking, eager
Emphat'ically, *ad.* ftrongly, forcibly, ftrikingly
Emphyfem'atous, *a.* bloated, fwelled, puffed up
Emp'ire, [Emp'ery,] *n.* imperial power, command,
Emp'iric, *n.* a pretended phyfician, a quack   (rule
Empir'ical, *a.* experimental, practiced by rote
Empir'ically, *ad.* experimentally, pretendedly
Empir'icifm, *n.* the practice or profeffion of quacks
Emplaft'er, *v. t.* to cover with a plafter
Emplaft'ic, *a.* vifcous, glutinous, clammy, tough
Employ', *v. t.* to keep at work, exercife, ufe, fpend
Employ', Employ'ment, *n.* bufinefs, a public office
Employ'able, *a.* fit to be employed or ufed
Employ'er, *n.* one who employs or fets to work
Enpoif'on, *v. t.* to poifon, to deftroy by poifon
Empoif'oner, *n.* one who poifons another perfon
Empórium, *n.* a feat of merchandife, a mart
Empov'erifh, *fee* Impoverifh
Empow'er, *v. t.* to authorife, to enable   (dignity
Emp'refs or Emp'erefs, *n.* a woman having imperial
Emprife, *n.* an attempt of danger, enterprife, *ob.*
Emp'tier, *n.* one who empties, one who makes void
Emp'tinefs, *n.* a void fpace, vanity, ignorance
Emp'tion, *n.* the act of buying, a purchafe
Emp'ty, *a.* void, unfurnifhed, *ignorant,* foolifh
Emp'ty, *v. t.* to exhauft, make void, deprive
Empur'ple, *v. t.* to make or dye of a purple color
Empuz'zle, *v. t.* to puzzle, perplex, confound, *ob.*
Empyr'eal, *a.* refined, beyond aerial, heavenly
Empyr'ean, *n.* the higheft heaven
Empyr'eum, *n.* the very higheft heaven or region
Empyreumat'ical, *a.* refembling burnt fubftances
Empyrófis, *n.* a general fire, a conflagration
Em'u, *n.* a very large bird of S. América, fix feet

K 2

Webster fit many brief definitions onto a single page of
*A Compendious Dictionary of the English Language.*

words with French-like spellings, such as *theatre* and *cheque,* to the more American-looking *theater* and *check.* These changes would be lasting ones. They would bring written English a little closer to the language Americans spoke.

Webster claimed that his *Compendious Dictionary* corrected faults in the dictionary of the great Samuel Johnson, especially Johnson's practice of citing Shakespeare. Webster had an opinion on just about every subject. Shakespeare, he thought, "was a man of little learning," whose language was "full of errors, and ought not to be offered as a model for imitation." He went through his own copy of Johnson's dictionary and made a black mark next to nearly every passage from Shakespeare.

John Quincy Adams was a U. S. senator when he questioned Webster's spelling reforms. He went on to serve as secretary of state under President James Monroe and to be elected president of the United States in 1824.

For a few months after the new dictionary appeared, Webster's enemies were silent. Then they released their barbs. "There is a time to write and a time to cease from writing," remarked an unnamed reviewer in the *Norfolk Register.* "Fortunate would it be for authors did they know when to terminate their labours."

Senator John Quincy Adams of Massachusetts questioned whether it made sense for the entire nation to change its rules of spelling based on "the authority of a single writer." What gave Noah Webster the right to decide for everyone else? About the new words in Webster's dictionary, Adams remarked, "There are always a multitude of words current within particular neighborhoods or during short periods of time, which ought never to be admitted into the legitimate vocabulary of the language." This future president preferred, he said, "to see them systematically excluded, rather than hunted up for admission into a Dictionary of classical English."

Webster paid to have a copy of the dictionary bound in leather and proudly sent it off to Thomas Jefferson, but the president never acknowledged the gift. Feeling persecuted and misunderstood, Webster compared himself to Galileo, who proved in the 1600s that the planets orbit the sun. He felt a kinship with the Italian scientist, who "was imprisoned by an ecclesiastical court, for defending the truth." And he kept on writing.

Around this time his daughter Julia came home from school to report that her teacher, Miss Hall, had shuttered the schoolhouse windows during a solar eclipse to keep her pupils safe. "I would not have you see it for the world," Miss Hall had declared when the Webster girls showed her the smoked glass their father had prepared to protect their eyes while viewing the spectacle. All New England had been waiting for the great event. A total solar eclipse had not been seen in the region since the time of English settlement, and many years would likely pass before one would be visible again. Yet the class sat inside a darkened schoolroom as the moon passed before the sun, casting the earth in shadow. An angry Webster announced to his family that such an ignorant and tyrannical teacher was unfit to instruct children. As one of the school's trustees, he made sure that Miss Hall was soon looking for a new post.

While battling the dunces who seemed to be everywhere, Webster was dealing privately with grief. His son Henry, who was born on November 26, 1806, died just nine weeks later. It was February, the bleakest month, when Henry was buried in New Haven's Grove Street Cemetery. Noah, Rebecca, and the little boy's sisters and brother mourned deeply. His loving father felt the pain of this loss for years to come.

For Noah Webster, words offered comfort. He produced another small dictionary, one meant to be used in common schools, but like the *Compendious Dictionary,* it was just a warm-up exercise. He was writing something grander and more significant, "a dictionary, which shall exhibit a far more correct state of the language than any work of this kind." He was determined to see the project through to the end, no matter what it required of him. "However arduous the task," he said, "and however feeble my powers of body and mind, a thorough conviction of the necessity and importance of the undertaking, has overcome my fears and objections."

The great project began on November 3, 1807. Unlike the esteemed Samuel Johnson, who had help from secretaries and scriveners, Webster worked alone. He hunted for words through the dictionaries, encyclopedias, and science books that lay spread open around his study. From the first light of morning until the day grew dim, he made notes to

Webster needed so much room to make notes beside the definitions in a Latin dictionary that he cut columns of words out of the book and glued them to a sheet of paper.

himself in the margins of these books and crafted the most accurate definitions he knew how to write. He worked standing up, because sitting was "an indolent habit," he said. At different times throughout the day he pressed his thumb to the opposite wrist and counted his pulse. Most often his heart beat sixty times per minute, but if he made an exciting discovery the number of beats rose to eighty or even eighty-five.

Such challenging work demanded quiet. The children's happy voices, the sweet sound of Rebecca calling to them, the clatter of a carriage passing in the street — any noise at all broke his concentration. Noah blocked himself off from the din of life by packing the walls of his study with sand. Yet there was one voice he found impossible to keep out: the one he believed belonging to God.

One morning in April 1808, he was alone in his study. "A sudden impulse upon my mind arrested me," he said. "I instantly fell on my knees, confessed my sins to God, implored him pardon, and made my vows to him that . . . I would live in entire obedience to his service." The next day he called his family together and led them in prayer, as he would do three times a day for the rest of his life.

Rebecca was overjoyed. She and the older girls had been attending services led by a zealous pastor named Moses Stuart, and she had been urging Noah to come along. Noah had resisted going with them, but now he did. Stuart preached a Calvinist doctrine that was much like the faith of Noah's and Rebecca's forebears. He taught that human beings are born sinful and must seek salvation through prayer and virtuous living.

Noah's new commitment to faith caused a rift in his friendship with Joel Barlow, who had rejected organized religion, although he did believe in a supreme being. Noah had promised to review Barlow's *Columbiad,* a newly published, expanded version of his *Vision of Columbus*. But he told

Barlow that he was changing his mind. Because the poem and its author promoted "atheistical principles," he could no longer write the review. He never understood how he hurt Joel's feelings by withdrawing his support, or why he then heard nothing from his old friend for two and a half years.

Having written his way through letters *A* and *B* of his great diction-ary, Webster took on another project, one inspired by his reading of the Bible. According to the book of Genesis, there was a time when all humans spoke a sin-gle language. Then some people built a sky-high structure called the Tower of Babel. It was so tall it reached into the clouds, nearly to heaven. Its build-ers gazed up at their great achievement and told one another that they were as powerful as God. But God disagreed. Angered by the people's arrogant pride, God scattered them to every part of the earth. Humanity no longer spoke one language, but many different tongues.

Webster aimed to reconstruct the original language from which, the Bible taught, all others had sprung. He be-gan studying twenty languages, from the Latin and Greek of his college

This illustration from an eighteenth-century Bible shows laborers constructing the Tower of Babel. According to the biblical story, at this time in history all people spoke a single language.

Twenty-two-year-old Emily Webster was engaged to be married when the family moved from New Haven to Amherst, Massachusetts.

years to Persian, Danish, and Welsh, comparing their words side by side. He planned to call his work "Synopsis of Words in Twenty Languages" and to make them part of his dictionary.

Experts in the new field of linguistics were using careful research to discover links between languages past and present—between ancient Sanskrit and modern Hindi, for example. Webster ignored these findings in favor of his own method. If any words in different languages sounded alike, he assumed they were historically connected, whether or not they actually were.

Unfortunately for Noah, none of this work brought in money. His earnings from his schoolbooks amounted to $2,400 a year. This was hardly enough to support his big family, which grew still larger with the birth of Louisa, the youngest child, in 1808. Noah wrote letter after letter—to friends, community leaders, college presidents, and politicians—asking for contributions to help fund his work on the great dictionary. Just seventeen people responded, sending him a total of $1,050—far too little. He estimated his need to be fifteen times as much. So he sent out more letters, to ministers, teachers, journalists, and printers, asking for only ten dollars from each. In return, donors could expect one day to receive a copy of Webster's dictionary, "on fine paper and in elegant binding." Again the replies barely trickled in.

Noah believed too strongly in his dictionary to give it up and find paying work. If there was no way to raise money, then he would cut his expenses. In July 1812, he sold the Benedict Arnold House and moved his family to the tiny town of Amherst, in the woods of western Massachusetts, where they could live cheaply and quietly.

Rebecca regretted leaving her friends in New Haven. Emily and Julia hated to move, because they were both in love. Emily was twenty-two and engaged to William Ellsworth, who was at Yale. He was the son of lawyer Oliver Ellsworth, with whom Noah had boarded years before. Julia, nineteen, was being courted by another Yale student, Chauncey Goodrich. As Noah's family climbed into the coach that was to carry them to their new home, both sisters were in tears. The gaiety of William and Eliza, who were eleven and nine, annoyed them no end. As the coach rolled under low-hanging trees, this happy pair reached out to catch at passing branches. To them, moving was pure adventure. "It was all new to us," Eliza said.

# CHAPTER 10

# THE SILENT CURRENT OF TIME

AMHERST IN 1812 was a village of white-painted wooden houses, each with a garden and outbuildings. Its two streets crossed near a common, a green space where the townspeople brought their cows to graze.

The Websters bought an eight-room house at one corner of the common, as well as ten adjoining acres, where Noah planted grape vines and fruit trees. People soon called his orchard the finest in town. He baled hay and milked the family's three cows, named Gentle, Comfort, and Crick. He sounded like his father when he shooed away neighborhood boys spotted loafing near his land: "Are you needed at home?" If a boy seemed willing to work, Noah hired him to help in the garden at twelve and a half cents an hour. "All the village boys grew fond of him," Eliza Webster said. "They would go down on purpose to be hired, for they liked the instruction he would give them about plants and trees, and grafting and budding, and they liked his wages also."

To Rebecca's delight, the Websters found new friends. Across the village green lived Pastor David Parsons, his wife, Harriet, and their eleven daughters and sons. On many a wintry night the Webster and Parsons girls entertained their families by performing religious plays.

In Amherst, Noah again used an upstairs room for his study. He claimed he had retired "to a humble cottage in the country," away from the din of politics and controversy. But the nation was at war, and he needed to be heard. In 1812

These illustrations from Noah Webster's book *Instructive and Entertaining Lessons for Youth* celebrate American agriculture and commerce. A farmer's son, Webster harvested hay on his land in Amherst.

the United States entered into conflict with Britain over its right to trade freely with other countries, including France, Britain's foe. The British had been seizing U.S. ships and forcing American seamen to fight for the Crown against France. After President James Madison declared war, battles broke out near the Canadian border; American soldiers died, including the twenty-five-year-old son of Noah's brother Abraham.

Then the Royal Navy stopped U.S. trade by blockading much of the Atlantic coast. This move especially hurt the merchants of New England, which is why many Federalists in the North opposed "Mr. Madison's War." The governors of Massachusetts and Connecticut refused to provide the army with militia forces, and the Massachusetts legislature urged men not to volunteer.

Most of the war's supporters in Congress came from states to the south and west, including the new states of Tennessee, Kentucky, and Louisiana, where slavery was legal. Counting the enslaved when determining how many representatives a state sent to Congress gave the South too much power, Webster and others claimed. "The southern states have an influence in our National Councils altogether disproportionate to their wealth, strength, and resources," Webster wrote. He and other Federalists wanted to change the Constitution to stop counting enslaved people, who had no vote and therefore no say in how they were governed. In his angriest moments Webster suggested that the United States be divided into three countries, North, South, and West.

The War of 1812 ended in December 1814 with no clear winner, before opponents like Webster could take any action. The three-fifths compromise would remain a point of controversy until 1865, when the Thirteenth Amendment to the Constitution abolished slavery throughout the United States.

Webster's joy at the coming of peace was dampened by sadness when

The War of 1812 was fought largely at sea. On August 19, 1812, USS *Constitution* battled a British warship, HMS *Guerriere,* on the Atlantic Ocean, four hundred miles southeast of Nova Scotia. This illustration shows the *Guerriere* defeated and nearly destroyed. U.S. forces rescued ten captured American seamen from among its crew.

he learned that Joel Barlow had died. His old friend had launched yet another career, that of a diplomat. In November 1812, the government sent Joel Barlow to Europe, to negotiate a trade agreement between the Americans and French. He caught up with the man then leading France, Napoleon Bonaparte, in Poland, where the French army was in retreat following a disastrous attack on Russia. Barlow came down with pneumonia and died in a Polish village on a cold December day. In 1813 Webster's eighty-year-old father died as well. By the time word reached Amherst, the funeral had already taken place.

Despite his wish to withdraw from the world and concentrate on his dictionary, Webster entered into the public debate on the War of 1812 and held public offices. This portrait is by the American artist James Herring.

In 1814 Webster was appointed justice of the peace. He had the authority to perform marriages and preside over minor court cases in the community. He served on the board of trustees of Amherst Academy, a school that opened in 1814. He was also elected to the first of three terms he was to serve in the Massachusetts House of Representatives. By 1816 he and Rebecca had three married daughters. Emily's love story had had a happy ending, and so had Julia's.

Emily and William Ellsworth were living in Hartford, where William would enter politics. Julia had married Chauncey Goodrich, who was teaching at Yale. Harriet's husband, Edward Cobb, was a wealthy merchant in Portland, Maine.

In 1817 Webster finished the "Synopsis," his tracing of the world's languages back to a single source, but he never published it. Like other biblical tales, the story of the Tower of Babel can be accepted on faith, but it is impossible to verify. The man who relied on facts had veered into guesswork.

And the great dictionary? Progress was slow, and money was running out. In 1816 Webster sold to the publisher Hudson and Company, for $23,000, the copyright to his spelling book, which was due for renewal in 1818. More and more copies of Webster's speller were being purchased every year, which meant that whoever held the copyright stood to earn a large profit over time. But again Webster could not wait. He wanted money then to support his family while he worked on his dictionary. He also needed to start fifteen-year-old William on his course in life, and the Hudsons had agreed to take the boy on as an apprentice clerk. If he worked hard, William could expect to be a partner in the firm one day.

Then, out of the blue, Webster was attacked in print by a linguist named John Pickering. It seemed that spelling changes Webster had put forth in his *Compendious Dictionary* were catching on, and this had Pickering upset. Americans were spelling *neighbor, favor, superior,* and other words without the *u* that was standard in England. Pickering also took issue with the American words Webster had defined. If words like *Americanize* and *boating* were not to be found in English dictionaries, then they had no place in American dictionaries either, according to Pickering. "The preservation of the *English language* in its purity throughout the United States is an object deserving the attention of every American," he wrote. After all, if American writers wanted their works read by the English, they needed to use language that the English could read with pleasure. Thirty years earlier, Pickering's father, Timothy Pickering, had purchased Webster's *Grammatical Institute* as the basis for his son's education. Now John Pickering said that Noah Webster seemed on a mission to "unsettle the whole of our admirable language."

Webster had grown sick and tired of controversy. "Rather than be engaged in it, I would spend the small portion of life that remains to me, in the humble walks of obscurity," he said. Yet he simply had to respond, and he did so by writing a pamphlet titled *A Letter to the Honorable John Pickering.* "In this country, new ideas, and associations of ideas, compel us, either to invent new terms, or to use English words in a new sense," he stated. Nouns take on new meanings as verbs; the noun *test* gave rise to the verb *to test,* for example. Some new words are formed by adding prefixes and suffixes to existing words; this was the way *Americanize* came into use. Existing words can also be used in new ways: "Thus, *smooth,* which, primarily, expresses the quality of a polished surface, has, by analogy, become a common word to express a like quality in language or style." He compared the evolution of language to "the motion of a broad river, which flows with a slow, silent, *irresistible* current." Finally, what did it matter if dictionaries in England omitted new American words? "New words will be formed and used, if found necessary or convenient," Webster concluded, "without a license from Englishmen."

In 1817 the Websters rejoiced in Mary's marriage to Horatio Southgate, a widower she had met while visiting Harriet in Maine. With the four oldest girls and William gone, the house in Amherst was quiet — too quiet even for Noah. Still, he and Rebecca Webster had known this day would come. They expected their children to have independent lives, except for Louisa, who was unable to live on her own. Whether Louisa had autism or was developmentally disabled is unclear, but she needed her parents' care and would remain with them.

But before long, William was back. Noah and Rebecca felt deep disappointment when Hudson and Company released their son from his apprenticeship and sent him home. "Hudson says that I take no interest in the business of the store, & that I am taken up with pleasure more than in business," William explained to his unhappy father.

There was more misfortune to come, as Noah discovered in 1818, when a letter arrived telling him that his younger brother, Charles, was dead. In February 1819, there was worse news: Mary Webster Southgate—Noah and Rebecca's beloved fourth child—had died following the birth of her daughter.

"Father opened the letter in our presence, turned pale, rose and left the room. Mother followed," Eliza remembered. "I crept to the bed room door and knocked gently. I heard sobbing and at last opened the door. Father knelt by the side of the bed—Mother close beside him." Eliza recalled with fondness Mary's "unwearied kindness to me and tender love. I was six years younger than Mary and shared her room after the marriage of my three elder, gifted sisters." Eliza remarked, "We were a changed household after this sore bereavement." Mary's grieving husband placed the infant, who was also named Mary, into the welcoming arms of her grandparents and asked them to raise her. This tiny, helpless link to their lost daughter brought Noah and Rebecca some consolation.

Could the Websters bear any more heartbreak? They would have no choice. Soon Harriet and Edward Cobb sailed to the West Indies, leaving their little girl to be cared for at home, in Portland. While in the islands Harriet and Edward both came down with yellow fever; Harriet pulled through, but the disease was fatal for Edward. A sorrowful Harriet made the long voyage home alone only to learn that her child had died while she was away. She returned to Amherst to live with her parents.

Time flowed on, silent and sure. Noah kept busy. He helped raise money to build a college in Amherst, which opened in 1821, with forty-seven students. He also plunged back into his dictionary. "With a humble dependence on Divine favor, for the preservation of my life and health, I shall prosecute the work with diligence, and execute it with a fidelity suited to its importance," he pledged. The problem was, though, that he could no longer work on the dictionary in remote Amherst. He needed input from brilliant minds—such as the professors at Yale. He needed to consult more books—like those housed in the library at Yale.

So he moved his household back to New Haven. Noah, Rebecca, William, Eliza, Louisa, Harriet, and little Mary Southgate lived in a rented house while having a new one built on Temple Street, near Julia and Chauncey Goodrich. Noah insisted that the carpenters construct a double wall around his second-floor study, where he would write and sleep. He made real progress on his dictionary; as 1823 neared its end, he was defining words starting with *R*.

Still, he wanted to dig deeper into words and their meanings. In old libraries in Europe, he knew, were books out of reach to scholars in America. If only he could run his eyes over their pages! Once the idea of traveling overseas formed in his mind, it gave him no peace. He simply had to go. On June 15, 1824, having borrowed a thousand dollars from his daughter Harriet, whose late husband had provided well for her, Noah boarded the *Edward Quesnel,* a ship sailing from New York to the port of Le Havre, France. William Webster went along as his father's assistant. Noah worried about William, who had enrolled at Yale but had earned poor grades and been asked to withdraw. At twenty-three, William drank too much and was in debt. He had left the church and seemed to be headed nowhere in life. Noah hoped this trip might set his son on a steady course.

The twenty-one passengers amused themselves with games of whist, chess, and dominoes, and gathered daily at three p.m. in the ship's dining hall for a lavish meal. On its third day at sea the *Edward Quesnel* sailed into a storm. As the vessel tossed one way and then another, many aboard, including William, took to their bunks with seasickness.

Not Noah; he was in awe of the wild weather. In a letter he described for Rebecca "the awful grandeur of a tempest at sea. To see the ocean rolling in mountains, foaming & roaring, & the wind howling, is a scene that may well appall the stoutest heart."

He wrote again to his dear Becca after coming ashore in Le Havre on July 10. "I cannot endure most of the dishes of French Cookery," he complained, yet he managed not to miss a meal, despite all the onions and garlic. "I have walked through the market," he continued, "& it is to me a great curiosity." He remarked on bareheaded women, some clanking about in wooden shoes, selling fish, vegetables, and foods for which he had no name. He spared Rebecca details that might have distressed her, such as the legion of rats that dwelled in this harbor city and the host of fleas that awaited sleepers in their hotel bedding.

The coach to Paris was like nothing father and son had ever seen. Called a diligence, it offered three compartments and seated fourteen passengers. All the passengers' luggage, which Noah estimated to weigh half a ton or more, was carried on top. William refused to be impressed. He called the diligence "a large clumsy wagon." Its six horses, he said, were "not fit for a plough," and their harnesses "would have disgraced the poorest beggars in America." The Webster men took rooms in a Paris lodging house, where the landlady cooked meals to suit their American tastes. "Today she had an excellent piece of beef roasted *a l'Americaine*, without onions and garlic, & really I seem to be at home," a satisfied Noah reported to Rebecca.

Noah's black clothes were as foreign in Paris as his love of plain cooking. Well-dressed Parisian men wore light-colored trousers held in place by straps that ran beneath their shoes. They favored top hats, soft cravats, and jackets with puffed sleeves and narrow waists. Some gentlemen squeezed into corsets to achieve the desired physique. An American who caught sight of Webster in Paris pegged him as "a curious, quaint, Connecticut looking apparition, strangely in contrast to the prevailing forms and aspects in this gay metropolis."

In the 1820s, stylish Parisian men wore top hats, fitted coats with full sleeves, and light-colored trousers held in place by straps that ran under the shoes. Webster stood out in his black New England wardrobe.

As soon as they were settled, Noah and William hurried to the Bibliothèque du Roi—the Royal Library—which was open to all. They stood under a high, vaulted ceiling and stared in wonder at shelves thirty feet tall, holding more than a million volumes and eighty thousand manuscripts. "I cannot give you a description of my feelings," Noah wrote to Becca. He spent six weeks poring over encyclopedias and dictionaries. He made pages of notes, which William copied in neat handwriting.

When not working, the two Websters toured Paris, which in 1824 was a city at peace. Noah especially loved the Jardin des Plantes (the botanical garden) and the National Museum of Natural History. "Every plant that will grow in the climate is here cultivated, & every species of animal from the whale, the camel & the elephant, to the smallest insect, is here found in a state of excellent preservation," he told his family at home. Though William had arrived in Paris quick to criticize, the city grew on him. "I know of no spot under Heaven where one could pass an earthly existence with more delight," he said.

When September came and the Royal Library closed for a month, Noah and William moved on to England. They settled in Cambridge so Noah could work at another historic research center, the Wren Library at Trinity College. He wrote to Rebecca that although he missed his family in New Haven, he was enjoying England: "It is a pleasant thing to get among people that look & dress & eat & talk like our own people."

Named for Christopher Wren, the architect who designed it in 1676, the Wren Library housed a smaller collection than that in the Royal Library in Paris, but Noah found plenty of information in its three hundred

Completed in 1695 and named for Sir Christopher Wren, the architect who designed it, the Wren Library today contains all the books Webster consulted there while completing his dictionary. The library's collection has grown since that time to include many more books and manuscripts of historical or literary importance.

thousand volumes. He labored in England for nearly five months, writing so much that he nearly wore out his right thumb. Finally, in late January 1825, he had just one more definition to write. Noah Webster was sixty-six years old and had looked forward to this moment for more than seventeen years. "I was seized with trembling which made it somewhat difficult to hold my pen steady for the writing," he said. "But I summoned strength to finish the last word." It was a scientific term: *zygomatic*.

# CHAPTER 11

# *"His Work Was Done"*

FROM CAMBRIDGE, Noah and William Webster traveled the short distance to London, where Noah tried to find someone to publish his dictionary. Its definitions included words in Hebrew, Arabic, and other foreign languages, and he worried that American publishers might not have all the different type fonts needed. Explaining that they already had large stocks of unsold dictionaries, one English publisher after another turned the project down. Father and son packed up the handwritten dictionary pages, and on May 18 they sailed back to the United States.

A month later, and more than a year after leaving home, they reached New Haven, where they were amazed by the welcome they received. Not only did Rebecca and the rest of the family rush to embrace them, but Yale's most esteemed professors and New Haven's leading citizens came out to greet them as well. It seems that scholars in Cambridge had written to their colleagues at Yale to tell them about Webster's

This is one of Webster's many handwritten manuscript pages. Before the invention of the typewriter in the mid-nineteenth century, all books had to be written by hand before being set into type.

gargantuan achievement. They told of one man, working virtually alone, who had crafted thorough, precise definitions for seventy thousand words and had included information on their etymology, or origins. It was a joyous time, and Noah's happiness only increased in July, when Harriet married again. Her second husband, the Reverend William Fowler, was the new pastor at a church in Amherst. Eliza also married a clergyman in 1825. Her husband, the Reverend Henry Jones, was a pastor in New Britain, Connecticut.

And there was more good news. Sherman Converse, editor of the *Connecticut Journal,* agreed to publish the dictionary. Webster still had work to do on it, though. He asked experts at Yale to check his scientific definitions for accuracy. He hired an assistant, James Gates Percival, to proofread the printed pages as they came off the press. Thirty years old, brilliant, and eccentric, Percival spoke ten languages fluently. He had begun his career as a physician, but he hated seeing patients, so he quit. He then became a chemistry professor, but he hated teaching, too, so he gave that up as well. When he met Webster he was living alone with his thousands of books. He wrote sentimental poetry and worked from time to time as a geologist.

Percival began the proofreading with excitement, but soon he wrote to a friend, "I regret that I have ever engaged in the thing." Not only was he putting in fourteen-hour days, but he and Webster had trouble getting along. It drove Webster crazy to see Percival wear the same old brown cloak every single day. If Percival looked up from his work and spotted Webster's frown, he knew what was coming. Webster was about to scold him for being sloppy; he was going to complain that Percival was making a mess of the pages. Well, Percival knew more than Webster did about some etymologies, or so he thought. He started making changes on his own, which threw Webster into a fury. In September 1828, having had enough, Percival quit.

By then almost all the work was done. Noah's head ached from it; he was cranky, and he jumped at every noise. The printer's eleven-year-old son, who carried the pages from the press to Temple Street, never saw the lexicographer smile. "He was a too-much pre-occupied man for frivolity, bearing, as he did, the entire weight of the English tongue upon his shoulders," the boy would later recall. The last pages were printed on November 26, 1828. The next day was Thanksgiving, and family members and friends filled the Webster home. They savored the feast Rebecca had cooked and congratulated Noah, who was finally ready to sit still and smile.

The great dictionary, so long in the making, was complete. As the news spread, Webster's critics sharpened their pens as if they were knives. They prepared with glee to slice the book and its author to pieces in their reviews. But when they got their hands on *An American Dictionary of the English Language,* they put away their blades. Anyone could see that Noah Webster had done something wondrous.

In two thick volumes Webster had defined every word of English used in America. He had explained terms from the worlds of mathematics and science, such as *conoid, datolite,* and *phosphorescent.* He had included everyday American terms, such as *chowder, underbrush, woodchuk,* and *Yankee*. In his definitions he offered brief, finely tuned discourses on the meanings of words, often followed by a quotation from literature or a sentence composed by himself, to show how the word was used. For example, he defined the noun LAND'SCAPE as "1. A portion of land or territory which the eye can comprehend in a single view, including mountains, rivers, lakes, and whatever the land contains." And, "2. A picture, exhibiting the form of a district of country, as far as the eye can reach, or a particular extent of land and the objects it contains, or its various scenery." He supplemented these definitions with a quote from poet John Milton:

> —*Whilst the* landscape *round it measures,*
> *Russet lawns and fallows gray,*
> *Where the nibbling flocks do stray.*

Having grown to expect insults and ridicule, Webster suddenly had to get used to praise. The editors of the *Connecticut Mirror* congratulated him "on the completion of his Herculean undertaking." His dictionary, they said, was a "vast monument of learning and industry." William Jay, son of John Jay, an author of the Federalist Papers and the first chief justice of the United States, wrote to Webster on behalf of his aged father. He stated that the dictionary "is a very valuable acquisition to our literature, & that it affords a proud proof of American talent & learning."

James L. Kingsley, a professor of Latin at Yale, wrote a long review of Webster's *American Dictionary*. Like the odd James Gates Percival, he questioned some of Webster's word origins. "In some cases the evidence on which the author has founded his opinions, is not very obvious," he wrote. In examining them he "experienced all the states of mind from full credence . . . to entire disbelief." Nevertheless, he told his readers, "The appearance of this dictionary, considering the circumstances under which it was begun, the amount of time and labor bestowed upon its composition, and the value of the improvements actually made, is an event upon which we may well congratulate the public." The worth of Webster's dictionary would "be seen in the better understanding of authors," Kingsley predicted. "It will be seen in the more correct use of words," he continued, and "in the increased respect, as we hope, with which the author will be viewed, for his talents, learning, and persevering industry."

Webster's dictionary fell short of perfection, as he was the first to admit. "This Dictionary, like all others of the kind, must be left, in some degree, imperfect; for what individual is competent to trace to their source, and define in all their various applications, popular, scientific and technical, *sixty* or *seventy thousand* words!" He wrote, "It satisfies my mind that I have done all that my health, my talents and my pecuniary means would enable me to accomplish." With *An American Dictionary of the English Language,* Webster had set a new standard of excellence. In the years, decades, and centuries to follow, he and others would refine and build on his glorious achievement.

The dictionary was Webster's gift to the United States and its people. "I present it to my fellow citizens, not with frigid indifference, but with my ardent wishes for their improvement and their happiness," he wrote,

Office, rank and great talents give *eminence* to men in society.

Where men cannot arrive at *eminence*, religion may make compensation, by teaching content.     *Tillotson.*

6. Supreme degree.     *Milton.*

7. Notice; distinction.     *Shak.*

8. A title of honor given to cardinals and others.     *Encyc.*

EM′INENT, *a.* [L. *eminens,* from *emineo.*]

1. High; lofty; as an *eminent* place. Ezek. xvi.

2. Exalted in rank; high in office; dignified; distinguished. Princes hold *eminent* stations in society, as do ministers, judges and legislators.

3. High in public estimation; conspicuous; distinguished above others; remarkable; as an *eminent* historian or poet; an *eminent* scholar. Burke was an *eminent* orator; Watts and Cowper were *eminent* for their piety.

EM′INENTLY, *adv.* In a high degree; in a degree to attract observation; in a degree to be conspicuous and distinguished from others; as, to be *eminently* learned or useful.

E′MIR, *n.* [Ar. اَمِير Emir, a commander, from اَمَرَ to command, Heb. אמר to speak, Ch. Syr. Sam. id.]

A title of dignity among the Turks, denoting a prince; a title at first given to the Caliphs, but when they assumed the title of Sultan, that of Emir remained to their children. At length it was attributed to all who were judged to descend from Mohammed, by his daughter Fatimah.     *Encyc.*

EM′ISSARY, *n.* [L. *emissarius,* from *emitto; e* and *mitto,* to send; Fr. *emissaire;* Sp. *emisario;* It. *emissario.*]

A person sent on a mission; a missionary employed to preach and propagate the gospel.

If one of the four gospels be genuine, we have, in that one, strong reason to believe, that we possess the accounts which the original *emissaries* of the religion delivered.     *Paley, Evid. Christ.*

[This sense is now unusual.]

2. A person sent on a private message or business; a secret agent, employed to sound or ascertain the opinions of others, and to spread reports or propagate opinions favorable to his employer, or designed to defeat the measures or schemes of his opposers or foes; a spy; but an *emissary* may differ from a *spy.* A *spy* in war is one who enters an enemy's camp or territories to learn the condition of the enemy; an *emissary* may be a secret agent employed not only to detect the schemes of an opposing party, but to influence their councils. A spy in war must be concealed, or he suffers death; an *emissary* may in some cases be known as the agent of an adversary, without incurring similar hazard.     *Bacon. Swift.*

3. That which sends out or emits. [*Not* used.]     *Arbuthnot.*

*Emissary vessels,* in anatomy, the same as *excretory.*

EM′ISSARY, *a.* Exploring; spying.     *B. Jonson.*

EMIS′SION, *n.* [L. *emissio,* from *emitto,* to send out.] The act of sending or throwing out; as the *emission* of light from the sun or other luminous body; the *emission* of odors from plants; the *emission* of heat from a fire.

2. The act of sending abroad or into circulation notes of a state or of a private corporation; as the *emission* of state notes, or bills of credit, or treasury notes.

3. That which is sent out or issued at one time; an impression or a number of notes issued by one act of government. We say, notes or bills of various *emissions* were in circulation.

EMIT′, *v. t.* [L. *emitto; e* and *mitto,* to send.]

1. To send forth; to throw or give out; as, fire *emits* heat and smoke; boiling water *emits* steam; the sun and moon *emit* light; animal bodies *emit* perspirable matter; putrescent substances *emit* offensive or noxious exhalations.

2. To let fly; to discharge; to dart or shoot; as, to *emit* an arrow. [*Unusual.*]     *Prior.*

3. To issue forth, as an order or decree. [*Unusual.*]     *Ayliffe.*

4. To issue, as notes or bills of credit; to print, and send into circulation. The United States have once *emitted* treasury notes.

No state shall *emit* bills of credit.     *Const. United States.*

EMMEN′AGOGUE, *n.* [Gr. εμμηνος, menstruous, or εν, in, and μην, month, and αγω, to lead.]

A medicine that promotes the menstrual discharge.     *Encyc.*

EM′MET, *n.* [Sax. *æmet, æmette;* G. *ameise.*] An ant or pismire.

EMMEW′, *v. t.* [See *Mew.*] To mew; to coop up; to confine in a coop or cage.     *Shak.*

EMMOVE′, *v. t.* To move; to rouse; to excite. [*Not used.*]     *Spenser.*

EMOLLES′CENCE, *n.* [L. *emollescens,* softening. See *Emolliate.*]

In metallurgy, that degree of softness in a fusible body which alters its shape; the first or lowest degree of fusibility.     *Kirwan.*

EMOL′LIATE, *v. t.* [L. *emollio, mollio,* to soften; *mollis,* soft; Eng. *mellow, mild;* Russ. *miluyu,* to pity; *umiliayus,* to repent. See *Mellow.*]

To soften; to render effeminate.

*Emolliated* by four centuries of Roman domination, the Belgic colonies had forgotten their pristine valor.     *Pinkerton, Geog.*

[This is a new word, though well formed and applied; but what connection is there between *softening* and *forgetting?* Lost is here the proper word for *forgotten.*]

EMOL′LIATED, *pp.* Softened; rendered effeminate.

EMOL′LIATING, *ppr.* Softening; rendering effeminate.

EMOL′LIENT, *a.* Softening; making supple; relaxing the solids.

Barley is emollient.     *Arbuthnot.*

EMOL′LIENT, *n.* A medicine which softens and relaxes, or sheaths the solids; that which softens or removes the asperities of the humors.     *Quincy. Coxe.*

EMOLLI′′TION, *n.* The act of softening or relaxing.     *Bacon.*

EMOL′UMENT, *n.* [L. *emolumentum,* from *emolo, molo,* to grind. Originally, toll taken for grinding. See *Mill.*]

1. The profit arising from office or employment; that which is received as a compensation for services, or which is annexed to the possession of office, as salary, fees and perquisites.

2. Profit; advantage; gains in general.

EMOLUMENT′AL, *a.* Producing profit; useful; profitable; advantageous.     *Evelyn.*

*Emongst,* for *among,* in Spenser, is a mistake.

EMO′TION, *n.* [Fr. from L. *emotio; emoveo,* to move from; It. *emozione.*]

1. Literally, a moving of the mind or soul; hence, any agitation of mind or excitement of sensibility.

2. In a *philosophical sense,* an internal motion or agitation of the mind which passes away without desire; when desire follows, the motion or agitation is called a *passion.*     *Kames' El. of Criticism.*

3. *Passion* is the *sensible effect,* the feeling to which the mind is subjected, when an object of importance suddenly and imperiously demands its attention. The state of absolute passiveness, in consequence of any sudden percussion of mind, is of short duration. The strong impression, or vivid sensation, immediately produces a reaction correspondent to its nature, either to appropriate and enjoy, or avoid and repel the exciting cause. This reaction is very properly distinguished by the term *emotion.*

*Emotions* therefore, according to the genuine signification of the word, are principally and primarily applicable to the sensible changes and visible effects, which particular *passions* produce on the frame, in consequence of this reaction, or particular agitation of mind.     *Cogan on the Passions.*

EMPA′IR, *v. t.* To impair. Obs. [See *Impair.*]

EMPA′LE, *v. t.* [Port. *empalar;* Sp. *id.;* It. *impalare;* Fr. *empaler; en, in,* and L. *palus,* It. Sp. *palo,* a stake, a *pale.*]

1. To fence or fortify with stakes; to set a line of stakes or posts for defense.

All that dwell near enemies *empale* villages, to save themselves from surprise.     *Raleigh.*

[We now use *stockade,* in a like sense.]

2. To inclose; to surround.

Round about her work she did *empale,* With a fair border wrought of sundry flowers.     *Spenser.*

3. To inclose; to shut in.

Impenetrable, *empal'd* with circling fire.     *Milton.*

4. To thrust a stake up the fundament, and thus put to death; to put to death by fixing on a stake; a punishment formerly practiced in Rome, and still used in Turkey.     *Addison. Encyc.*

EMPA′LED, *pp.* Fenced or fortified with stakes; inclosed; shut in; fixed on a stake.

EMPA′LEMENT, *n.* A fencing, fortifying or inclosing with stakes; a putting to death by thrusting a stake into the body.

2. In botany, the calyx or flower-cup of a

---

Its careful, complete definitions and commentary from the author make Webster's 1828 dictionary a joy to read even today.

"and for the continued increase of the wealth, the learning, the moral and religious elevation of character, and the glory of my country."

Webster's *American Dictionary* sold well enough, despite its hefty price of twenty dollars, for Noah and Rebecca to enjoy financial security. On October 26, 1829, they celebrated their fortieth wedding anniversary with a turkey dinner. They reflected on their lives, their seven grown children, and the many grandchildren Noah now delighted with his flute. "Few have jogged on together more harmoniously," Rebecca said. Noah thought too about the family he had grown up with in Hartford, and in the summer he visited his brother Abraham, who was nearly eighty. It was to be their last meeting; Abraham died the next year.

Noah himself was more than seventy years old, but he was as hard-working as ever. He produced two abridged editions of his *American Dictionary* for use in homes and schools, a British edition, a collection of brief biographies for schoolchildren, and an updated version of the *American Spelling Book*. In late December he traveled to Washington, D.C., with his daughter Emily and her husband. William Ellsworth had been elected to Congress as a representative from Connecticut.

Washington was now a thriving city of nineteen thousand people, with too many houses for one old man to count. People there knew about Webster and his dictionary, and it gladdened Noah to be welcomed by members of government. John Marshall, chief justice of the Supreme Court, told him, "There are few if any of us who do not possess your large dictionary, and who do not entertain a just opinion of its merits." Senators and congressmen informed Webster that they had learned to read from

Rebecca Greenleaf Webster's portrait was painted late in her life by an unknown artist.

his schoolbooks. Since 1804, Webster's spelling book had been bound in a blue paper cover. People spoke of it fondly as the "blue-backed speller." "I know of nothing that has given me more pleasure in my journeys," he wrote to his son-in-law William Fowler, "than the respect and kindness manifested towards me in consequence of the use of my books."

He was invited to the White House, where he sat to the right of President Andrew Jackson during dinner. In Webster's view, Jackson's belief in a small federal government and his support of slavery made him as bad as Jefferson. His tough, combative nature and spotty education made him even worse. But Webster for once kept his opinions to himself and took in the scene around him. Thirty distinguished guests sat at a dining table graced by gilt urns filled with artificial flowers. "The president was very sociable," he reported to his daughter Harriet. "We had a great variety of dishes, French and Italian cooking," he noted, "to the great annoyance of American guests." On January 3, 1831, Webster lectured in the House of Representatives, and at last an audience was eager to hear him. He spoke on his favorite subject, the English language. He also urged the congressmen to extend the term of an author's copyright beyond fourteen years. A month later Jackson signed into law an act that lengthened the term of a copyright to twenty-eight years with an option to renew it for another fourteen.

Before leaving Washington, Webster patched up his friendship with his brother-in-law James Greenleaf. After leaving prison James had married again and worked hard to restore his fortune and his good name. He was living in a mansion near the U.S. Capitol.

But books and writing were Webster's business, and he was eager to get back to work. He had no plans to retire. "I am so accustomed to action that I presume inaction would be tedious & perhaps not salutary," he said. He credited his good health to vigorous walks, plenty of vegetables, and small amounts of meat, without "oil and other French dressings."

Having written a dictionary, he turned to the Bible. The King James Version, the Bible in widest use in North America, was an English translation of the sacred texts published during the reign of King James I of England. Webster found its language beautiful in its simplicity. Many of its words, however, had fallen into disuse or had taken on new meanings since 1611, when the King James Version first appeared. Webster felt a moral duty to make corrections. "Whenever words are understood in a sense different from that which they had when introduced, and different from that of the original languages," he explained, "they do not present to the reader the *Word of God.*" He went through the Bible and substituted *evening* for *even-tide,* for example, *cows* for *kine,* and *perhaps* for *peradventure.* If he spotted grammatical errors — if, for instance, the original authors of the King James Version used *which* when they should have used *who* — he corrected these "mistakes" too. Finally, he substituted

Elected the seventh president of the United States in 1828, Andrew Jackson rose to prominence as the army general who defeated the British in the Battle of New Orleans, the last military engagement of the War of 1812.

milder terms for the "indelicate words and phraseology, which decency does not permit to be uttered in company," as when he replaced *fornication* with *lewdness*. Some Yale professors endorsed Webster's Bible, but most Americans continued to buy the King James Version, which they preferred.

One reason Noah kept writing was to employ William as an assistant. He was still trying to turn his son's life around. William had failed at teaching school before going to Virginia to tutor a rich man's sons. He lasted only a short while in the post, but he fell in love with his employer's sister, a young woman named Rosalie Stuart, and married her in May 1831. Noah loaned William

The Websters' only surviving son, William, drifted from one line of work to another. In the years to come his marriage would fail, and his two sons would die in the Civil War, one fighting for the North and the other for the South.

money that never was repaid; his daughters begged him to stop helping William and force him to manage for himself.

Noah also worried about Harriet, who was showing signs of tuberculosis. Fretful, exhausted, and in pain, Harriet often took to her bed. To lighten her workload, she sent the oldest of her four children, Emily, to stay with Noah and Rebecca for a year. Noah delighted in this "hopping, dancing, waltzing, chattering" twelve-year-old who loved books and could read and write Latin. During her year in New Haven, Emily Fowler formed happy memories of a doting grandfather who would stop the carriage, if they went for a drive, so she could climb down and pick flowers.

Ever a teacher, Webster compiled another reading book for America's schoolchildren, *Instructive and Entertaining Lessons for Youth*. In 1841 he published a new edition of his dictionary that included fifteen thousand more words than the previous one. He also gathered essays he had written over the past fifty years, and in 1843 he issued them as a book, *A Collection of Papers on Political, Literary and Moral Subjects*.

The Websters' granddaughter Emily Fowler grew up to be a writer. Using her married name, Emily Fowler Ford, she published poetry, essays, and a two-volume biographical memoir, *Notes on the Life of Noah Webster*.

At eighty-four Webster still walked two or three miles a day. He was "remarkably erect throughout life, and moving, even in his advanced years, with a light and elastic step," observed his son-in-law Chauncey Goodrich. This was why his daughter Eliza was so concerned when she peeked into his study on the afternoon of May 24, 1843, and caught sight of him wrapped in a shawl and lying down. He complained of being tired and feeling a chill. The family called in a physician, who examined the old man and diagnosed pleurisy, an inflammation of the membrane surrounding the lungs. Two days later Eliza noted, "Our solicitude for dear father is very *great*. He is *very sick*." The pleurisy had progressed to pneumonia.

Noah's family gathered around him. Rebecca was at his side, and so were William Webster and Julia and Chauncey Goodrich. Emily and William Ellsworth came from Hartford, where they had been living since William was elected governor of Connecticut in 1838. Eliza, who was acting as her father's nurse, was already staying in the Temple Street house. Pas-

The picture of Webster that appeared in his 1828 dictionary was based on a portrait painted by Samuel F. B. Morse, who is best remembered for inventing the electronic telegraph and Morse code.

tor Moses Stuart came as soon as he could. There was no time to send word to Harriet in Amherst, but even if there had been, ill health might have prevented her from traveling. Harriet died of tuberculosis the following year.

"It soon became necessary to inform him that he was in imminent danger," wrote Chauncey Goodrich. "He received the communication with surprise, but with entire composure. His health had been so good, and every bodily function so perfect in its exercise, that he undoubtedly expected to live some years longer." Noah told his loved ones that he had enjoyed his long life because he had filled it with useful labor. To his old friend Pastor Stuart he spoke of his confidence in God.

On the night of Sunday, May 28, Eliza wrote, "All is over. Father, dear father, has gone to rest. . . . He said his work was *done,* and he was *ready.*"

# EP'ILOGUE

noun. a conclusion; the closing part of a discourse.

NOAH WEBSTER wrote millions of words on myriad subjects: education, the English language, the government and the Constitution, life in New York City, and yellow fever, to name a few. Some of the issues he wrote about evoke strong opinions even today. Twenty-first-century Americans still disagree about how much power the federal government should have. They are divided on the need for all Americans to speak English. They ask, should schools and other institutions offer services in Spanish and other languages? Also, with Americans looking for ways to improve U.S. schools, some people call for a national system of education.

As technology offers innovations and culture changes, people invent words that end up in dictionaries. *Defriend, flash mob, blog, ringtone, gastric bypass, drama queen*—these and other new terms have found their way into everyday speech and into print. Their appearance in dictionaries draws comments just like those Noah Webster heard: "This makes me worry about the future of the English language"; "I just lost all hope in humanity."

Today people remember Noah Webster best for his most ambitious work, *An American Dictionary of the English Language*. After Webster died, George and Charles Merriam, two brothers living in Springfield, Massachusetts, bought the rights to his great dictionary. Having hired Chauncey Goodrich as an editor, the G. and C. Merriam Company published its first revised edition of the dictionary in 1847. The Merriams then brought in experts to refine Webster's etymologies and scientific definitions. Their 1859 edition defined 140,000 words and was the first dictionary to have illustrations. In 1890 the Merriams issued a still larger edition, *Webster's International Dictionary of the English Language*. The name Webster came to mean "dictionary" to many Americans. When they wanted to know the meaning of a word, they spoke of looking it up in "Webster's."

By this time the Merriams' copyright had expired. This meant that anyone could publish a dictionary and tack the name "Webster's" onto the title. The Merriam Company went to court and obtained a ruling that required these other books to state in print: "This dictionary is not published by the original publishers of Webster's Dictionary or by their successors."

For many years, though, Webster's most popular work was his spelling book. The Merriams acquired the rights to the spelling book in 1857,

Noah Webster's face has been placed over a page of the manuscript for his great dictionary in this late nineteenth-century print. The open book is an 1890 edition of *Webster's International Dictionary*. To the right is Webster's blue-backed speller, which was renamed *The Elementary Spelling Book* in 1829.

and D. Appleton and Company of New York did the printing for them. In 1880 William H. Appleton said that "Webster's Speller" was the firm's best-selling book. "We sell a million copies a year," he boasted. The small blue-backed speller had found its way, Appleton said, "to every cross-roads store in the country." Children learned from it in one-room sod schoolhouses on the prairie, in the mining settlements of Colorado and Nevada, and in newly built towns in California that smelled of fresh lumber.

"Above all books which have united us in the bond of common language, I place the good old Spelling-Book of Noah Webster," Jefferson Davis, a U.S. senator from Mississippi, has been quoted as saying in 1859. "We have a unity of language no other people possesses, and we owe this unity, above all else, to Noah Webster's Yankee Spelling-Book." Three years later, Davis was president of the Confederate States of America, a nation formed by the southern states that had broken away from the Union and were fighting against the United States in the Civil War. Unity of language had not been enough to hold the country together. Issues that had divided Americans since the Constitution was drafted—whether the federal government ought to have power over the states, and whether the United States should permit slavery—had festered and had led to the split. The reunited nation that emerged in 1865, after the U.S. victory in this war, was one with a strong federal government, in which slavery was outlawed. Noah Webster would have approved.

Sales of Webster's spelling book jumped to a million and a half copies in the year after the Civil War, when many African Americans, newly freed from slavery, were learning to read. But as the nineteenth century ended and the twentieth began, sales declined. More American children were learning to read from the McGuffey Readers, a new series of textbooks, than from the blue-backed speller. But teachers still used Webster's book for spelling lessons and spelling bees.

In 1883, a century after Webster published his first speller, a poet named Joel Benton recalled the quaint little book. He described the triumph he felt as a boy when he mastered Webster's simple sentences, such as "She fed the old hen" and "Ann can hem my cap." Nothing he learned later "would ever seem so touching and significant," he confessed. On Webster's spelling book "there rests now a gleam and fascination that no poet or novelist can give, or ever gave," Benton wrote. "It is the twilight halo tinting the first far boundary of youth; and restores now a little glimpse, almost, of a pre-existent world."

# *Notes*

vii    Epigraph: Webster, "Life is short . . .": Rudolph, *Essays on Education,* 46.

**Begin'ning**

1    Webster, "I am not formed . . .": and "The reflections of my own mind": *Rollins, Autobiographies of Noah Webster,* 83.

2    "incurable lunatic": Lepore, "Noah's Mark," 80.

2    "spiteful viper": "Vain, Ostentatious Noah Webster," 24.

3    Webster, "America is an independent empire . . .": Webster, *Sketches of American Policy,* 47.

3    Webster, "So long as any individual state . . .": Ibid., 32.

3    Webster, "It is the business of *Americans* . . .": Webster, *Grammatical Institute,* vol. 1, 15.

3    "this oddity of literature": Unger, *Life and Times of Noah Webster,* 248.

4    Webster, "*A* is the first letter . . .": Webster, *American Dictionary,* vol. 1, unnumbered page.

## 1. A Boy Who Dreamed of Books and Words

6    Webster, "the sound of a little hollow . . .": Rollins, *Autobiographies of Noah Webster*, 199.

9    Dilworth, "ba be bi bo bu": Dilworth, *New Guide*, 2.

9    Dilworth, "No Man may put off . . .": Ibid., 5.

10    "that ould deluder . . .": Johnson and Reed, eds., *Historical Documents in American Education*, 7.

10    "of a pale complexion . . .": Elsbree, *American Teacher*, 26–27.

10    Webster, "in idleness, in cutting tables . . .": Unger, *Life and Times of Noah Webster*, 9.

12    Frye, "This horrid scene . . .": Dodge, *Relief Is Greatly Wanted*, 92.

15    Webster, "considerable degree of knowledge . . ." *Connecticut Courant*, August 20–27, 1771, 4.

15    Webster, "from the envious and ilnatur'd": Ibid.

17    Waldo, "an intelligent and agreeable companion . . .": Sprague, *Annals of the American Pulpit*, 3–4.

17    Perkins, "sinless perfection": Perkins, *Twenty-Four Discourses*, viii.

17    Perkins, "the right way . . .": Ibid., vii.

18    Webster, "To his instruction and example . . .": Webster, "Dr. Nathan Perkins," 36.

## 2. College in Wartime

20    "very much decayed": Cowle, *Educational Problems at Yale College*, 11.

22    Trumbull, "of no advantage . . .": Trumbull, *Essay on the Use and Advantages of the Fine Arts*, 3.

22    "His mind was rapid . . ." Parker, *Discourse Occasioned by the Death of the Rev. Joseph Buckminster*, 10.

22 "Frankness and honesty . . .": Ibid.

22 "deep gloom of mind": Ibid., 16.

23 "All the Scholars are required . . .": *Laws of Yale-College,* 5.

24 "If any Scholar shall any where act . . .": Ibid., 11.

24 "Poise your firelock . . .": Goodyear, "Some Historic Yale Letters," 799.

25 "a little salt-water tea": Drake, *Tea Leaves,* cxxxviii.

25 Deane, "in high spirits . . .": *Collections of the Connecticut Historical Society,* 169.

27 Fitch, "filled the country . . .": Durfee, "Memoir of Rev. Ebenezer Fitch," 358.

27 Washington, "I heard the bullets whistle . . .": Ford, *Writings of George Washington,* 90.

27–28 Webster, "expressed their surprise . . ." and "It fell to my humble lot . . .": Rollins, *Autobiographies of Noah Webster,* 118.

30 Paine, "Of more worth . . .": Paine, *Common Sense,* 18.

31 Webster, "The musketoes were so numerous . . .": Unger, *Life and Times of Noah Webster,* 24.

31 Webster, "The very air . . .": Rollins, *Autobiographies of Noah* Webster, 120.

33 Webster, "Terror and devastation . . .": Rollins, *Autobiographies of Noah Webster,* 121.

34 Webster, "Burgoyne is taken . . .": Ibid.

34 Webster, "An army of British regulars . . .": Ibid.

35 "Ignorance of the Middle Ages . . ." and Stiles, "disputed inimitably well": Dexter, *Literary Diary of Ezra Stiles,* 284.

35 Webster, "nature has a peculiar . . .": Webster, "Short View of the Origin and Progress," 384.

36 Webster, "The human mind . . .": Ibid., 338.

36    Barlow, "We are not the first men . . .": Hill, *Joel Barlow,* 18.

**3. Seeking a Living**

37    Noah Webster, Sr., "You must now seek . . .": Rollins, *Autobiographies of Noah Webster,* 133.

38    Webster, "Set afloat in the world . . .": Ibid., 98.

38    Johnson, "The safe and general antidote . . .": Johnson, *Rambler,* 108.

39    Barlow, "I have too much confidence . . .": Todd, *Life and Letters of Joel Barlow,* 18.

40    "Who is that young man . . .": Flanders, *Lives and Times of the Chief Justices,* 63.

43    Webster, "The practice of law . . .": Unger, *Life and Times of Noah Webster,* 34.

43    Webster, "Young Gentlemen and Ladies . . .": advertisement in the *Connecticut Courant and Weekly Intelligencer,* June 5, 1781, 3.

44    Webster, "That education is always *wrong* . . .": Webster, *Collection of Essays and Fugitiv Writings,* 28.

45    Smith, "reflections are as prosy . . .": Monaghan, *Common Heritage,* 25.

45    Webster, "improvement of the human mind": "The Tablet," 477.

45    Barlow, "all the majesty of nature . . .": Barlow, *A Poem, Spoken,* 7.

46    "firm league of friendship": *Articles of Confederation,* March 1, 1781. Available online through the Avalon Project: avalon.law.yale.edu/18th_century/artconf .asp. Downloaded on January 6, 2013.

47    Deane, "Will our commerce flourish . . .": Deane, *Paris Papers,* 9.

47    Deane, "the jarring interests . . .": Ibid., 44.

48    Webster, "The perpetual opposition . . ." and "The unlimited advantage . . .": Webster, "Observations on the Revolution of America," 2.

49    "the cowboy of the Ramapos": Shart, *Land O' Goshen,* 13.

50    Webster, "Every State in America . . .": Webster, *Grammatical Institute,* vol. 1, 5.

50    Webster, "a flat drawling . . .": Ibid., 7.

50    "Let us make it as familiar . . .": Feer, *Shay's Rebellion,* 41.

## 4. A New Book to Teach a New Nation

51    Webster, "extreme depression," and "gloomy forebodings": Rollins, *Autobiographies of Noah Webster,* 47.

51    Webster, "The principal part of instructors . . ."; and "some easy guide . . .": Webster, *Grammatical Institute,* vol. 1, 6.

52    Webster, "Nothing has a greater tendency . . .": Ibid., 12.

52    Webster, "One half of the work . . .": Ibid., 10.

52    Webster, "the spelling book does more . . .": Webster, *Collection of Papers on Political,* 309.

54    Webster, "would a child or a foreigner . . .": Webster, *Grammatical Institute,* vol. 1, 5.

54    Webster, "Be not wise . . .": Ibid., 103.

55    Barlow, "old Dilworth . . .": Todd, *Life and Letters of Joel Barlow,* 42.

57    Madison, "impertinent fops": Ketcham, *James Madison,* 52.

58    Webster, "printing, publishing & vending": Monaghan, *Common Heritage,* 27.

59    Noah Webster, Sr., "I rejoyce to hear . . .": Ford, *Notes on the Life of Noah Webster,* vol. 1, 56.

60    Webster, "However some may think . . ." and "like a star . . .": Warfel, *Letters of Noah Webster,* 4.

61    Continental Congress, "new books, not hitherto printed": Rudd, "Notable Dates in American Copyright, 1783–1969."

62    Webster, "no printer or bookseller . . ."; "destitute of the means . . ."; "his fortitude never forsook him"; and "generosity far exceeded his ability": Rollins, *Autobiographies of Noah Webster,* 139.

63    Webster, "an easy, concise and systematic Method . . .": *Connecticut Courant,* September 16, 1783, 2.

63    Webster, "The celebrated Spelling-Book . . ." and "a scarecrow . . .": *Connecticut Courant, and Weekly Intelligencer,* October 14, 1783,1.

63    Webster, "the public to examine . . .": Ibid.

64    Webster, "Every grammar that was ever written . . .": Warfel, *Letters of Noah Webster,* 13.

64    Webster, "a bare-faced assertion!": Ibid., 14.

64    Webster, "was christened by the gentleman . . .": Ibid., 20.

64    Webster, "I have too much pride . . .": Ibid., 31.

65    Massachusetts legislature, "calculated to raise . . .": Bacon, *Supplement to the Acts and Resolves,* 180.

65    Webster, "Congress and the bold patriots . . .": Rollins, *Autobiographies of Noah Webster,* 195.

66    Webster, "When people . . . have delegated . . ." and "no matter whether it be right . . .": *Connecticut Courant, and Weekly Intelligencer,* September 30, 1783, 1.

66    Webster, "A refusal to comply . . ." *Connecticut Courant, and Weekly Intelligencer,* September 2, 1783, 2.

66    Webster, "ended in smoke": Rollins, *Autobiographies of Noah Webster,* 140.

66    Webster, "A happy event!": Ibid., 196.

## 5. Lonely Traveler

68    Webster, "Could I have kept my copyright . . .": Monaghan, *Common Heritage,* 82.

68    Webster, "Had a fine Partner . . .": Rollins, *Autobiographies of Noah Webster,* 197.

68    Webster, "pulled twenty ways . . .": Ibid., 194.

69    Webster, "I have lived long enough . . .": Ibid., 203.

69   "The dreams of congress . . .": Hutchinson and Stedman, *Library of American Literature,* 423.

70   Webster, "Let every state . . .": Webster, *Sketches of American Policy,* 44.

70   Webster, "the general voice . . .": Ibid., 6.

70   Webster, "All power is vested . . .": Ibid., 31.

70   Webster, "a complete knowledge . . .": Webster, *Grammatical Institute,* vol. 3, 3–4.

70   Day, "attack upon the safety . . .": Ibid., 179.

71   Webster, "regular features . . .": Ibid., 89.

71   Webster, "plunged in calamities . . .": Rollins, *Autobiographies of Noah Webster,* 211.

71   Greene, "The spirit of building . . .": Chappelle, *Baltimore,* 46.

72   Webster, "The General burst out . . .": Rollins, *Autobiographies of Noah Webster,* 123.

73   Webster, "very social": Kendall, *Forgotten Founding Father,* 3.

73   Webster, "two or three hundred . . ." and "not recovered . . .": Rollins, *Autobiographies of Noah Webster,* 346.

73   Webster, "A shame to Virginia!": Ibid., 347.

74   Webster, "O how disagreeable!": Ibid.

74   Webster, "They behave with great decency . . ."; "remarkably attentive . . ."; and "Charleston is very regular": Ibid., 215.

75   "production of a native . . .": Warfel, *Noah Webster,* 123.

76   Webster, "People in Baltimore . . ." and "sweeps us away!": Rollins, *Autobiographies of Noah Webster,* 218.

77   Webster, "American Dr. Moyes": Kendall, *Forgotten Founding Father,* 113.

77   Webster, "The English language . . .": Ibid., 114.

78    Webster, "Some of the southern people . . .": Webster, *Dissertations on the English Language,* 110.

78    Webster, "It seems to be . . .": Ibid.

78    Webster, "gross impropriety"; "pronounce a *t* . . ."; and "*oncet* and *twicet* . . .": Ibid., 111.

78    Webster, "a habit of laughing . . ." and "our political harmony . . .": Ibid., 20.

78    Webster, "generally pronounced *deef* . . ." Ibid., 128.

79    Webster, "from time immemorial": Ibid.

79    "appears to be enraptured . . .": Morgan, *Noah Webster,* 100.

79    "know-it-all": Kendall, *Forgotten Founding Father,* 114.

79    "what are commonly called . . .": Warfel, *Letters of Noah Webster,* 49.

79    Webster, "I wish to express . . .": Ibid., 48.

79    Timothy Pickering, "I am determined . . .": Pickering, *Life of Timothy Pickering,* 480.

81    Rush, "Education alone . . .": Butterfield, *Letters of Benjamin Rush,* 388–89.

81    Webster, "Sir, you may congratulate . . .": Warfel, *Noah Webster,* 160.

81    Webster, "The Ladies will not dance . . .": Rollins, *Autobiographies of Noah Webster,* 224.

81    Webster, "Its excellence consists . . .": Webster, *Collection of Essays and Fugitiv Writings,* 389.

## 6. A Friend to His Country

82    Webster, "to seek a living . . .": Kendall, *Forgotten Founding Father,* 135.

82    Webster, "not designed for *amusement* . . .": Warfel, *Noah Webster,* 159.

83    Webster, "the depraved taste": *New Hampshire Spy,* February 16, 1787, 135.

83    Seth, "consciousness of his own great learning . . ."; "extraordinary knowledge

and abilities"; and *"to wit*, that of a schoolmaster": *Freeman's Journal,* April 18, 1787, 3.

83    Webster, "the noblest that can actuate . . ." and "This may be strange . . .": *Freeman's Journal,* April 25, 1787, 2.

83    Noah Webster, Sr., "I have had a hint . . .": Ford, *Notes on the Life of Noah Webster,* vol. 1, 174.

84    Webster, "Any scheme for introduction . . .": Rollins, *Autobiographies of Noah Webster,* 147.

86    Webster, "dear Becca," and "sweet girl": Warfel, *Letters of Noah Webster,* 68.

86    Webster, "revive your image . . .": Ibid, 70.

86    Webster, *"Without you . . ."*: Ibid., 68.

88    Morris, "the curse of heaven . . .": Adams, *Gouverneur Morris,* 160.

90    Webster, "I know of no other . . .": Warfel, *Letters of Noah Webster,* 261.

90    Fitzsimmons, "as a friend . . .": Rollins, *Autobiographies of Noah Webster,* 148.

90    Webster, "I firmly believe . . ." and "Congress will have no more power . . .": Webster, *An Examination of the Leading Principles,* 29.

90    Webster, "Perfection is not the lot . . .": Ibid., 52.

90    Webster, "the perfection of human government": Ibid., 7.

91    Webster, "A principal bulwark . . .": Ibid., 49.

92    Webster, "to gratify every class . . ." and "Ribaldry and immoral writings . . .": *American Magazine,* January 1788, 3.

93    Webster, "The only practicable method . . ." and "Education should therefore be . . .": Unger, *Life and Times of Noah Webster,* 142.

94    Curiosus [Webster], "whether a man . . ." and "to become acquainted . . .": *American Magazine,* January 1788, 109.

94    Webster, "The most convenient and agreeable . . .": Webster, "General Description of New York City," 221.

94 Webster, "New-York is one of the most social . . ." and "great inconvenience . . .": Ibid., 225.

94 Noah Webster, Sr., "I think they are well written . . .": Unger, *Life and Times of Noah Webster,* 144.

## 7. Coxcomb General of the United States

95 Webster, "The march was slow . . .": Webster [writing as Pratt], "Federal Procession," 2.

96 Webster, "his excellency General Washington . . .": Ibid.

98 Webster, "30 years of my life . . .": Rollins, *Autobiographies of Noah Webster,* 259.

99 Webster, "It is now the work . . ." and "Most people remain . . .": Webster, *Dissertations on the English Language,* 396.

99 Webster, "All persons, of every rank . . ." and "Such a uniformity . . .": Ibid., 397.

99 Webster, "a great Philosopher . . .": Ibid., iii.

100 Franklin, "an excellent work . . .": Franklin, *Memoirs of Benjamin Franklin,* 620.

101 Webster, "A saving of an eighteenth . . .": Webster, *Dissertations on the English Language,* 397.

102 Webster, "If there ever was a woman . . .": Ford, *Notes on the Life of Noah Webster,* vol. 1, 206–7.

102 Webster, "This day I became . . .": Rollins, *Autobiographies of Noah Webster,* 270.

103 Greenleaf, "That you may live *long* . . .": Ford, *Notes on the Life of Noah Webster,* vol. 1, 273.

103 Rebecca Webster, "eleven pumpkins puddings . . ." Ibid., 270–71.

104 Rebecca Webster, "Mr. Webster's mother . . .": Ibid.

104 Webster, "one of the greatest blessings . . .": Webster, *American Dictionary of the English Language,* vol. 2, unnumbered page.

105 Webster, "Peeces . . . ritten at various times . . ." and "appeared before in periodical papers . . .": Webster, *Collection of Essays and Fugitiv Writings,* ix.

106    Belknap, "*No-ur Webster eskwier . . .*": Unger, *Life and Times of Noah Webster,* 165.

106    Webster, "doubtful . . . whether the public mind . . .": Ibid.

106    Webster, "A Prompter then says but *little* . . ." and "The writer of this little Book . . .": Webster, *Prompter,* unnumbered page.

107    Webster, "What a wise man . . .": Ibid., 51.

107    Webster, "When a man is going. . . ." and "First, it is much easier . . .": Ibid., 49.

107    Webster, "sowing *wild oats*" and "Habit sticks fast . . .": Ibid., 59.

## 8. Compiler of Facts

110    Webster, "creating some evils . . .": Unger, *Life and Times of Noah Webster,* 177.

110    "*Vive* Ge-nêt!": Ibid., 186.

110    Webster, "I cannot with propriety . . .": Ford, *Notes on the Life of Noah Webster,* vol. 1, 373.

112    "with keen gray eyes . . .": Lamb, *History of the City of New York,* 454.

112    "Many householders deem it so useful . . .": *American Minerva,* December 9, 1793, 1.

112    Webster, "Never will the brave freemen . . .": Snyder, *Defining Noah Webster,* 127.

113–114    Webster, "Becca is compelled . . ." and "Thanks to my good fortune . . .": Kendall, *Forgotten Founding Father,* 196.

116    Webster, "As *facts* are the basis . . .": Webster, *Collection of Papers on the Subject of Bilious Fevers,* iv.

116    Webster, "The world is a book. . .": Unger, *Life and Times of Noah Webster,* 209.

116    Webster, "Is not a partial delirium . . .": Ibid., 212.

116    Webster, "It is as much the *duty* . . .": Webster, *Collection of Papers on the Subject of Bilious Fevers,* 239.

117 Webster, "I am fatigued . . .": Morgan, *Noah Webster,* 139.

117 Webster, "My plan of education . . .": Warfel, *Letters of Noah Webster,* 142.

119 Webster, "Such is my progress . . .": Kendall, *Forgotten Founding Father,* 238.

120 Webster, "Facts which were new . . .": Webster, *Brief History of Epidemic and Pestilential Diseases,* ix.

121 Webster, "The spot where this fever arose . . .": Ibid., 348.

121 Webster, "All America Mourns": Rollins, *Autobiographies of Noah Webster,* 323.

123 Steele, "Have you completed . . .": Kendall, *Forgotten Founding Father,* 239.

## 9. Mixing Weeds and Flowers

124 Webster, "on account of differences . . .": Kendall, *Forgotten Founding Father,* 232.

124 Webster, "a living language": Webster, *Compendious Dictionary of the English Language,* xxiii.

124 Webster, "must keep pace . . .": Webster, *Letter to the Honorable John Pickering,* 28.

125 "mortal and incurable lunatic": Lepore, "Noah's Mark," 80.

125 "turn his mind . . .": Kendall, *Forgotten Founding Father,* 232.

125 "If, as Mr. Webster asserts . . .": Lepore, "Noah's Mark," 79.

125 Webster, "Either from the structure . . ." and "withdraw myself . . .": Warfel, *Letters of Noah Webster,* 248.

126 Johnson, "to meet face to face . . .": McAdams and Milne, *Johnson's Dictionary,* 39.

127 Webster, "In groping thro the dark labyrinth . . .": Webster, *Miscellaneous Papers on Political and Commercial Subjects,* 46.

127 Webster, "Your administration will sink you . . .": Ibid., 49.

128 Webster, "To what a state . . .": Ibid., 20.

128    Jefferson, "I view Webster . . .": Ford, *Works of Thomas Jefferson,* 285.

128    Webster, "The field of inquiry . . .": Warfel, *Letters of Noah Webster,* 319.

130    Webster, "was a man of little learning . . .": Boulton, *Johnson,* 134–35.

130    "There is a time to write . . .": Kendall, *Forgotten Founding Father,* 256.

131    Adams, "the authority of a single writer" and "There are always a multitude of words . . .": Unger, *Life and Times of Noah Webster,* 256.

131    Webster, "was imprisoned by an ecclesiastical court . . .": Boulton, *Johnson,* 125.

131    Hall, "I would not have you see it . . .": Ford, *Notes on the Life of Noah Webster,* vol. 1, 454.

132    Webster, "a dictionary, which shall exhibit . . ." and "However arduous the task . . .": Webster, *Compendious Dictionary of the English Language,* xxiii.

133    Webster, "an indolent habit": Webster, *Collection of Essays and Fugitiv Writings,* 392.

134    Webster, "A sudden impulse upon my mind . . .": Rollins, *Autobiographies of Noah Webster,* 51.

135    Webster, "atheistical principles": Hill, *Joel Barlow,* 89.

137    Webster, "on fine paper . . .": Warfel, *Letters of Noah Webster,* 280.

137    Eliza Webster, "It was all new . . .": Ford, *Notes on the Life of Noah Webster,* vol. 2, 108.

## 10. The Silent Current of Time

138    Webster, "Are you needed at home?" and Eliza Webster, "All the village boys . . .": Ford, *Notes on the Life of Noah Webster,* vol. 2, 169.

139    Webster, "to a humble cottage . . .": Micklethwait, *Noah Webster and the American Dictionary,* 159.

140    "Mr. Madison's War": Boller, *Presidential Campaigns,* 26.

140    Webster, "The southern states . . .": Unger, *Life and Times of Noah Webster,* 278.

143   John Pickering, "The preservation of the *English language* . . .": Pickering, *Vocabulary or Collection of Words and Phrases,* 2.

144   John Pickering, "unsettle the whole . . .": Ibid., vi.

144   Webster, "Rather than be engaged . . .": Webster, *Letter to the Honorable John Pickering,* 34.

144   Webster, "In this country . . .": Ibid., 8.

144   Webster, "Thus, *smooth* . . .": Ibid., 7.

144   Webster, "the motion of a broad river . . .": Ibid., 29.

144   Webster, "New words will be formed . . .": Ibid., 7.

145   William Webster, "Hudson says that I take no interest . . .": Monaghan, *Common Heritage,* 162.

145   Eliza Webster, "Father opened the letter . . ." and "unwearied kindness to me . . .": Ford, *Notes on the Life of Noah Webster,* vol. 2, 167.

146   Webster, "With a humble dependence . . .": Webster, *Compendious Dictionary of the English Language,* xxiii.

147   Webster, "the awful grandeur . . .": Ford, *Notes on the Life of Noah Webster,* vol. 2, 199.

147   Webster, "I cannot endure . . .": Ibid., 207.

148   Webster, "I have walked . . .": Ibid., 208.

148   William Webster, "a large clumsy wagon": Warfel, *Noah Webster,* 354.

148   Webster, "Today she had . . .": Ford, *Notes on the Life of Noah Webster,* vol. 2, 212.

148   "a curious, quaint, Connecticut looking apparition . . .": Goodrich, *Personal Recollections,* 480.

150   Webster, "I cannot give you a description . . .": Ford, *Notes on the Life of Noah Webster,* vol. 2, 213.

150   Webster, "Every plant that will grow . . .": Ibid., 222.

150 William Webster, "I know of no spot . . .": Kendall, *Forgotten Founding Father,* 297.

150 Webster, "It is a pleasant thing . . .": Monaghan, *Common Heritage,* 107.

151 Webster, "I was seized with trembling . . .": Ford, *Notes on the Life of Noah Webster,* vol. 2, 293.

## 11. "His Work Was Done"

154 Percival, "I regret that I have ever engaged . . .": Micklethwait, *Noah Webster and the American Dictionary,* 197.

155 "He was a too-much pre-occupied man . . .": *Ohio Archaeological and Historical Publications,* 315.

156 Webster, "1. A portion of land . . ." and Milton, "—Whilst the landscape . . .": Webster, *American Dictionary of the English Language,* unnumbered page.

156 "on the completion . . .": "Webster's American Dictionary," *Connecticut Mirror,* January 31, 1829, 3.

156 Jay, "is a very valuable acquisition . . .": Micklethwait, *Noah Webster and the American Dictionary,* 198.

157 Kingsley, "In some cases the evidence . . ." and "experienced all the states of mind . . .": Kingsley, "Webster's Dictionary," 456.

157 Kingsley, "The appearance of this dictionary . . ." and "be seen in the better understanding . . .": Ibid., 478.

157 Webster, "This Dictionary, like all others . . ." and "I present it . . .": Webster, *American Dictionary of the English Language,* unnumbered page.

159 Rebecca Webster, "Few have jogged on . . .": Kendall, *Forgotten Founding Father,* 309.

159 Marshall, "There are few . . .": Hobson, ed. *Papers of John Marshall,* vol. 12, 14.

160 Webster, "I know of nothing . . .": Micklethwait, *Noah Webster and the American Dictionary,* 217.

161 Webster, "The president was very sociable . . .": Ibid., 216.

161  Webster, "I am so accustomed . . .": Snyder, *Defining Noah Webster,* 278.

162  Webster, "oil and other French dressings": "Noah Webster," 567.

162  Webster, "Whenever words are understood . . .": Webster, *Holy Bible,* iii.

163  Webster, "indelicate words and phraseology . . .": Webster, *Instructive and Entertaining Lessons for Youth,* 2.

164  Webster, "hopping, dancing . . .": Kendall, *Forgotten Founding Father,* 322.

164  Goodrich, "remarkably erect . . .": Goodrich, "Memoir of Noah Webster," xxii.

165  Jones, "Our solicitude . . .": Kendall, *Forgotten Founding Father,* 327.

165  Goodrich, "It soon became necessary . . .": Goodrich, "Memoir of Noah Webster," xxii.

166  Jones, "All is over . . .": Kendall, *Forgotten Founding Father,* 328.

**Ep'ilogue**

168  "This makes me worry . . ." and "I just lost all hope . . .": *Oxford Dictionaries.*

168  "This dictionary is not published . . .": Micklethwait, *Noah Webster and the American Dictionary,* 305.

169  Appleton, "We sell a million copies . . .": Monaghan, *Common Heritage,* 193.

170  Davis, "Above all books . . .": Unger, *Life and Times of Noah Webster,* 343.

171  Webster, "She fed the old hen": Webster, *Elementary Spelling Book,* 19.

171  Webster, "Ann can hem my cap . . .": Ibid., 21.

171  Benton, "would ever seem . . .": Benton, "Webster Spelling-Book," 306.

# Selected Bibliography

Adams, William Howard. *Gouverneur Morris: An Independent Life*. New Haven, Conn.: Yale University Press, 2003.

Bacon, Edward Monroe. *Supplement to the Acts and Resolves of Massachusetts*. Vol. 1: *1780–1784*. Boston: George H. Ellis, 1896.

Barlow, Joel. *A Poem, Spoken at the Public Commencement at Yale College, in New-Haven, September 12, 1781*. Hartford, Conn.: Hudson and Goodwin, 1781.

Benton, Joel. "The Webster Spelling-Book." *Magazine of American History*, 1883, pp. 299–306.

Boller, Paul F., Jr. *Presidential Campaigns: From George Washington to George W. Bush*. New York: Oxford University Press, 2004.

Boulton, James T., ed. *Johnson: The Critical Heritage*. New York: Barnes and Noble, 1971.

Burstein, Andrew. *Sentimental Democracy: The Evolution of America's Romantic Self-Image*. New York: Hill and Wang, 1999.

Butterfield, L. H., ed. *Letters of Benjamin Rush*. Vol. 1: *1761–1792*. Princeton, N.J.: Princeton University Press, 1951.

Chappelle, Suzanne Ellery Greene. *Baltimore: An Illustrated History.* Sun Valley, Calif.: American Historical Press, 2000.

*Collections of the Connecticut Historical Society.* Vol. 2. Hartford, Conn.: Connecticut Historical Society, 1870.

Cowie, Alexander. *Educational Problems at Yale College in the Eighteenth Century.* New Haven, Conn.: Yale University Press, 1936.

Deane, Silas. *Paris Papers.* New York: James Rivington, 1782.

Dexter, Franklin Bowditch, ed. *The Literary Diary of Ezra Stiles, D.D.* New York: Charles Scribner's Sons, 1901.

Dilworth, Thomas. *A New Guide to the English Tongue.* 13th ed. London: Henry Kent, 1751.

Dodge, Edward J. *Relief Is Greatly Wanted: The Battle of Fort William Henry.* Bowie, Md.: Heritage Books, 1998.

Drake, Francis S. *Tea Leaves: Being a Collection of Letters and Documents Relating to the Shipment of Tea to the American Colonies in the Year 1773.* Boston: A. O. Crane, 1884.

Durfee, Calvin. "Memoir of Rev. Ebenezer Fitch." *American Quarterly Register,* 1843, pp. 353–78.

Elliott, John, and Samuel Johnson, Jr. *A Selected Pronouncing and Accented Dictionary.* Suffield, Conn.: Oliver D. and I. Cook, 1800.

Elsbree, Willard. *The American Teacher: Evolution of a Profession in a Democracy.* New York: American Book Co., 1939.

Feer, Robert A. *Shay's Rebellion.* New York: Garland, 1988.

Flanders, Henry. *The Lives and Times of the Chief Justices of the Supreme Court.* Vol. 2. New York: James Cockcroft and Co., 1875.

Ford, Emily Ellsworth, comp. *Notes on the Life of Noah Webster.* New York: privately printed, 1912.

Ford, Paul Leicester, ed. *The Works of Thomas Jefferson.* Vol. 9. New York: G. P. Putnam's Sons, 1904–5.

Ford, Worthington Chauncey, ed. *The Writings of George Washington*. Vol. 1: *1748–1757*. New York: G. P. Putnam's Sons, 1889.

Franklin, Benjamin. *Memoirs of Benjamin Franklin*. Vol. 1. New York: Derby and Jackson, 1859.

Friend, Joseph H. *The Development of American Lexicography, 1798–1864*. The Hague, Netherlands: Mouton, 1967.

Goodrich, Chauncey. "Memoir of Noah Webster," in *A Dictionary of the English Language* by Noah Webster. Springfield, Mass.: G. and C. Merriam, 1870.

Goodrich, S. G. *Personal Recollections of Poets, Philosophers and Statesmen*. New York: Arundel, 1856.

Goodyear, A. C. "Some Historic Yale Letters Edited from the Manuscripts in His Own Collection." *Yale Alumni Weekly*, April 9, 1926, pp. 799–801.

Hill, Peter P. *Joel Barlow: American Diplomat and Nation Builder*. Washington, D.C.: Potomac Books, 2012.

Hobson, Charles F., ed. *The Papers of John Marshall*. Vol. 12. Chapel Hill: University of North Carolina Press, 2006.

Hutchinson, Ellen Mackay, and Edmund Clarence Stedman, eds. *A Library of American Literature from the Earliest Settlement to the Present Time*. Vol. 3. New York: William Everts Benjamin, 1884.

Johnson, Samuel. *The Rambler*. London: J. M. Dent and Sons, 1953.

Johnson, Tony W., and Ronald F. Reed, eds. *Historical Documents in American Education*. Boston: Allyn and Bacon, 2002.

Kelley, Brooks Mather. *Yale: A History*. New Haven: Yale University Press, 1974.

Kendall, Joshua. *The Forgotten Founding Father: Noah Webster's Obsession and the Creation of an American Culture*. New York: G. P. Putnam's Sons, 2010.

Ketcham, Ralph. *James Madison: A Biography*. Charlottesville: University Press of Virginia, 1990.

Kilbourne, Payne Kenyon. *Sketches and Chronicles of the Town of Litchfield, Connecticut*. Hartford, Conn.: Case, Lockwood and Co., 1859.

Kingsley, James L. "Webster's Dictionary." *North American Review,* April 1829, pp. 433–79.

Lamb, Martha J. *History of the City of New York: Its Origin, Rise and Progress.* Vol. 2. New York: A. S. Barnes and Co., 1880.

*The Laws of Yale-College.* New Haven, Conn.: Thomas and Samuel Green, 1774.

Lepore, Jill. "Noah's Mark: Webster and the Original Dictionary Wars." *New Yorker,* November 6, 2006, pp. 78–87.

McAdams, E. L., Jr., and George Milne, eds. *Johnson's Dictionary: A Modern Selection.* Mineola, N.Y.: Dover Publications, 2005.

Micklethwait, David. *Noah Webster and the American Dictionary.* Jefferson, N.C.: McFarland and Co., 2000.

Monaghan, E. Jennifer. *A Common Heritage: Noah Webster's Blue-Back Speller.* Hamden, Conn.: Archon Books, 1983.

Morgan, John S. *Noah Webster.* New York: Mason/Charter, 1975.

"Noah Webster." *New Englander,* October 1843, pp. 565–68.

*Ohio Archaeological and Historical Publications.* Vol. 4. Columbus: Ohio State Archaeological and Historical Society, 1895.

*Oxford Dictionaries: Language Matters.* Available online. URL: blog.oxforddictionaries .com/2013/08/new-words-august-2013. Downloaded on April 11, 2014.

Paine, Thomas. *Common Sense: Addressed to the Inhabitants of America.* New York: Peter Eckler, 1918.

Parker, Nathan. *A Discourse Occasioned by the Death of the Rev. Joseph Buckminster, D.D.* Portsmouth, N.H.: S. Whidden, 1812.

Perkins, Nathan. *Twenty-Four Discourses on Some of the Important and Interesting Truths, Duties and Intuitions of the Gospel.* Hartford, Conn.: Hudson and Goodwin, 1795.

Pickering, John. *A Vocabulary or Collection of Words and Phrases Which Have Been Supposed to Be Peculiar to the United States.* New York: Burt Franklin Reprints, 1974.

Pickering, Octavius. *The Life of Timothy Pickering.* Vol. 1. Boston: Little, Brown, and Co., 1867.

Rankin, Hugh F. *The Theater in Colonial America.* Chapel Hill: University of North Carolina Press, 1965.

Rollins, Richard M. *The Autobiographies of Noah Webster: From the Letters and Essays, Memoir, and Diary.* Columbia: University of South Carolina Press, 1989.

Rudd, Benjamin W., comp. "Notable Dates in American Copyright, 1783–1969." United States Copyright Office. Available online: www.copyright.gov/history/dates.pdf. Downloaded on February 15, 2013.

Rudolph, Frederick, ed. *Essays on Education in the Early Republic.* Cambridge, Mass.: Belknap Press, 1965.

Shart, Elizabeth. *Land O' Goshen: Then and Now.* Paterson, N.J.: Quality Press, 1960.

Snyder, K. Alan. *Defining Noah Webster: A Spiritual Biography.* Washington, D.C.: Allegiance Press, 2002.

Sprague, William B. *Annals of the American Pulpit; or Commemorative Notices of Distinguished American Clergymen of Various Denominations.* Vol. 2. New York: Robert Carter and Brothers, 1866.

"The Tablet." *Gazette of the United States,* June 2–16, 1790, pp. 474–90.

Todd, Charles Burr. *Life and Letters of Joel Barlow, LL.D., Poet, Statesman, Philosopher.* New York: G. P. Putnam's Sons, 1886.

Trumbull, John. *An Essay on the Use and Advantages of the Fine Arts.* New Haven, Conn.: T. and S. Green, 1770.

Unger, Harlow Giles. *The Life and Times of Noah Webster, an American Patriot.* New York: John Wiley and Sons, 1998.

"Vain, Ostentatious Noah Webster." *Milwaukee Journal,* October 4, 1945, p. 24.

Warfel, Harry R. *Noah Webster: Schoolmaster to America.* New York: Macmillan, 1936.

————, ed. *Letters of Noah Webster.* New York: Library Publishers, 1953.

Weaver, Glenn. *Hartford: An Illustrated History of Connecticut's Capital.* Woodland Hills, Calif.: Windsor Publications, 1982.

Webster, Noah. *An American Dictionary of the English Language.* New York: S. Converse, 1828.

_____. *A Brief History of Epidemic and Pestilential Diseases.* Vol. 1. Hartford, Conn.: Hudson and Goodwin, 1799.

_____. *A Collection of Essays and Fugitiv Writings.* Boston: I. Thomas and E. T. Andrews, 1790.

_____. *A Collection of Papers on Political, Literary, and Moral Subjects.* New York: Webster and Clark, 1843.

_____. *A Collection of Papers on the Subject of Bilious Fevers.* New York: Hopkins, Webb and Co., 1796.

_____. *A Compendious Dictionary of the English Language.* Hartford, Conn.: Hudson and Goodwin, 1806.

_____. *A Dictionary of the English Language.* Springfield, Mass.: G. and C. Merriam, 1870.

_____. *Dissertations on the English Language.* Boston: Isaiah Thomas and Co., 1789.

_____. "Dr. Nathan Perkins." *Boston Recorder,* March 2, 1838, p. 36.

_____. *The Elementary Spelling Book.* New York: American Book Co., 1908.

_____. *An Examination of the Leading Principles of the Constitution Proposed by the Late Convention Held at Philadelphia.* Philadelphia: Prichard and Hall, 1787.

_____ [writing as Richard Pratt], "Federal Procession, in Honor of the Constitution of the United States." *New-York Daily Advertiser,* August 2, 1788, pp. 1–3.

_____. "General Description of New York City." *American Magazine,* March 1788, pp. 221–25.

_____. *A Grammatical Institute of the English Language.* 3 vols. Hartford, Conn.: Hudson and Goodwin, 1783–85.

_____. *The Holy Bible, Containing the Old and New Testaments, in the Common Version.* New Haven, Conn.: Durrie and Peck, 1833.

_____. *Instructive and Entertaining Lessons for Youth.* New Haven, Conn.: S. Babcock and Durrie and Peck, 1835.

_____. *A Letter to the Honorable John Pickering, on the Subject of His Vocabulary.* Boston: West and Richardson, 1817.

_____. *Miscellaneous Papers on Political and Commercial Subjects.* New York: E. Belden and Co., 1802.

_____. "Observations on the Revolution of America." *New-York Packet, and the American Advertiser,* January 17, 1782, p. 2; January 31, 1782, p. 2; and February 7, 1782, p. 2.

_____. *The Prompter: A Commentary on Common Sayings Which Are Full of Common Sense, the Best Sense in the World.* Newport, N.H.: John Wilcox, 1833.

_____. "A Short View of the Origin and Progress of the Science of *Natural Philosophy.*" *New-York Magazine; or, Literary Repository,* June-July 1790, pp. 338–40 and 383–84.

_____. *Sketches of American Policy.* Hartford, Conn.: Hudson and Goodwin, 1785.

"Webster's American Dictionary." *Connecticut Mirror,* January 31, 1829, p. 3.

# The Major Works
# of Noah Webster

*A Grammatical Institute of the English Language.* 3 vols. Hartford, Conn.: Hudson and
Goodwin, 1783–85.

*Sketches of American Policy.* Hartford, Conn.: Hudson and Goodwin, 1785.

*An Examination of the Leading Principles of the Constitution Proposed by the Late Conven-
tion Held at Philadelphia.* Philadelphia: Prichard and Hall, 1787.

*Dissertations on the English Language.* Boston: Isaiah Thomas and Co., 1789.

*A Collection of Essays and Fugitiv Writings.* Boston: I. Thomas and E. T. Andrews, 1790.

*The Prompter; or, A Commentary on Common Sayings and Subjects.* Boston: I. Thomas and
E. T. Andrews, 1792.

*A Collection of Papers on the Subject of Bilious Fevers.* New York: Hopkins, Webb and
Co., 1796.

*A Brief History of Epidemic and Pestilential Diseases.* Hartford, Conn.: Hudson and
Goodwin, 1799.

*Elements of Useful Knowledge.*

> Volume 1: *Containing a Historical and Geographical Account of the United States.*
> Hartford, Conn.: Hudson and Goodwin, 1802.

Volume 2: *Containing a Historical and Geographical Account of the United States.* New Haven, Conn.: Sidney's Press, 1804.

Volume 3: *Containing a Historical and Geographical Account of the Empires and States in Europe, Asia and Africa, with Their Colonies.* New Haven, Conn.: Bronson, Walter and Co., 1806.

Volume 4: *History of Animals.* New Haven, Conn.: Howe and Deforest, and Walter and Steele, 1812.

*A Compendious Dictionary of the English Language.* Hartford, Conn.: Hudson and Goodwin, 1806.

*A Dictionary of the English Language, Compiled for the Use of Common Schools in the United States.* New York: Brisban and Brannan, 1807.

*An American Dictionary of the English Language.* New York: S. Converse, 1828.

*Biography, for the Use of Schools.* New Haven, Conn.: H. Howe, 1830.

*History of the United States.* New Haven, Conn.: Durrie and Peck. 1832.

*The Holy Bible, Containing the Old and New Testaments, in Common Version.* New Haven, Conn.: Durrie and Peck, 1833.

*Instructive and Entertaining Lessons for Youth.* New Haven, Conn.: S. Babcock and Durrie and Peck, 1835.

*A Collection of Papers on Political, Literary and Moral Subjects.* New York: Webster and Clark, 1843.

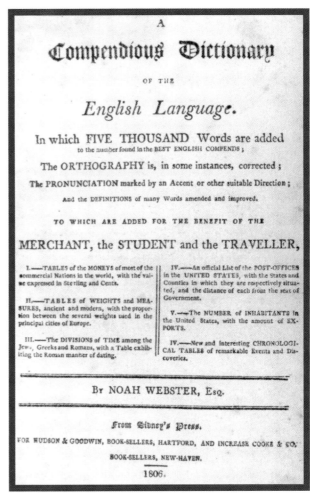

This is the title page from *A Compendious Dictionary of the English Language.* Webster's first dictionary was published in 1806.

# Picture Credits

# Index

Page numbers in **bold** type denote illustration and photo captions.